Listening Prayer

LEARNING TO HEAR
THE SHEPHERD'S VOICE

Listening Prayer

LEARNING TO HEAR
THE SHEPHERD'S VOICE

JOANNE HILLMAN

WhiteFire Publishing

WhiteFire Publishing
13607 Bedford Rd NE
Cumberland, MD 21502

ISBNS: 978-1-939023-14-8 (print)
         978-1-939023-15-5 (digital)

There are many people who...speak to God
in prayer,
but hardly even listen to Him,
or else listen to Him only vaguely.

~ Paul Tournier (1898~1986)

CHAPTER 1

Learning to Listen

MY SHEEP LISTEN TO MY VOICE;
I KNOW THEM, AND THEY FOLLOW ME.
~ JOHN 10:27

"Father, what do You want me to know?" I wrote in my journal. Did I really want to know what God had to say to me? My life was far from perfect, my Christian walk often wayward, and I was more than a little afraid of direct conversation with Him. I tried to quiet my mind, almost an impossible task. After a few moments, I picked up my pen and began to write: *I love you. I have been with you through all the hard times of your life, loving and upholding you. You cannot imagine how much I care for you.*

Amazed, I stared at the paper. The words were in my handwriting, but these were not my thoughts. I would never have expressed myself in this way. Those words remain some of the most precious, the most healing ones ever spoken to me. Even now, tears spring to my eyes when I read them again.

How often had God wanted to convey this message of love

to me?

What is He even now waiting to tell you?

What exactly is listening prayer?

"Listening prayer" is a way to bring His guidance into our everyday walk by expanding our prayers into two-way conversations. This may seem almost an oxymoron if we have always understood prayer to mean going to God with a list of our requests. As we look back, however, most of us can remember times when we received strong impressions that could only have come from Him, and those experiences have changed our lives.

Too often, our prayers amount to a monologue, much like the story Nicky Gumbel tells in his delightful video and book, *Questions of Life*.[1] A man went to his physician with an entire list of complaints. "My shoulder hurts, and I have this cough that won't go away, and I often have blinding headaches, and sometimes my left knee locks, and my back hurts a lot." Then, without waiting for a response, he says, "Thank you very much, doctor," and leaves. How can the physician help you unless you wait and listen to his response? It's ludicrous to waste your time and his without waiting to hear his recommendations. You'd consider your office visit terribly incomplete.

Our prayers are too often the same as this man's doctor visit—only half-finished—unless we wait for God's response.

Listening prayer is a simple tool to help us hear God's voice by using a daily journal, recording not only our own prayers, but also the answers He lays upon our hearts.

How I began listening

Several years ago I lived and worked at Hidden Manna Christian Retreat Center in New Waverly, Texas, under the direction of Dr. Paul Looney, one of the finest Christians I've ever known. As a staff member, I attended many excellent conferences held at the center. At one of these, Dr. Looney invited Dave Olson of El Cajon, California, to teach the basics of the prayer journaling technique he and his wife Linda developed.[2]

Skeptical at first, I was astonished to realize that God would speak to the likes of me. Even more amazing was how my untrained, wayward spirit could recognize His voice so clearly that I could write His words on paper. Since then, my prayer journals have become treasures, second only to my Bible.

My relationship with God has changed as a result. Now I know, and I know that I know, I am His beloved child. He delights in my coming to Him with anything, anytime I wish.

During John F. Kennedy's presidency, a touching incident happened at the White House that illustrates this new relationship. While President Kennedy met with several other heads of state, into this important conference ran his small daughter, Caroline, calling, "Daddy, Daddy."

He turned away from his guests and held welcoming arms toward her. Before she reached him, she tripped and fell, crying in pain. President Kennedy picked her up, held her in his arms, and kissed her tears away.

I, too, can run to my Father, the Creator and King of the Universe, whenever I wish. I don't need an intermediary, nor do I need to come hanging my head in fear. Whatever special business He is about, He always has time for me. I can bring all my questions to Him and receive wisdom. He guides me through conflict and teaches me how to mend fractured relationships. He takes the veil away from my eyes and helps me understand His Word. His love shines through the pages of my journal, so that even His correction is sweet. He cares enough for me not to let me remain in my wrong thinking and judgmental attitudes.

I'm sure there is much more transformation ahead. More hard times and struggles will have to be overcome. But I know He will lead me, guide me, encourage me, and comfort me as I meet with Him daily for our wonderful dialogue.

Does God want to talk with us?

Relationship is the most important reason for hearing the voice of the Lord. God is not only infinite, but also personal. If we don't have communication, we don't have a personal relationship with Him. True guidance is getting close to the Guide. We grow to know the Lord better as He speaks to us. As we listen to Him and obey Him, we make His heart glad.[3]

Requirements

Our first need is to recognize Jesus as the Son of the Living God, crucified for our sins, resurrected and living forever as Lord of Lord and King of Kings. This is the gate to a relationship with God (John 14:6). Any other entrance is that of a thief and a robber (John 10:1). If you have not yet made the decision to submit to His lordship, the prayer of commitment at the end of this book will guide you in this step. This is the most important and life-transforming decision you will ever make. You can be sure He will meet you with open arms.

When He sees us turn to Him, like the father of the prodigal son, He runs to us, rejoicing (Luke 20:21). And all heaven rejoices! (Luke 15:10).

Resist the enemy if he tries to tell you that your commitment is not real. The very name of Jesus is powerful. James 4:7 says we need only resist Satan, and he will flee like the coward he is.

We must search our hearts as we come before God (Psalm 19:14) and confess any sin we find there. His Word says He will not hear us unless our hearts are pure (Psalm 66:18).

How will I hear Him?

Usually, God speaks to us through His living, breathing

Word, ever revealing His will and His nature. He may speak through a particular verse as we follow our daily Bible study. The Bible tells of His speaking to Moses in an audible voice (Exodus 3:4). He gave dreams and visions to the Wise Men and to Joseph (Matthew 2). Isaiah and the Apostle John were given visions (Isaiah 6:1; Revelation 1:12-17). But the most common way is through His still, small voice speaking to our hearts (Isaiah 30:21) as the Bible resonates with our yielded hearts.

As we continue coming to Him as little children, presenting our questions and problems, recognizing God's voice will become easier. But we must remember that our obedience is essential. Like strong-willed lambs, if we wander away from the sound of our Shepherd's voice, danger awaits us. If we cannot hear Him, perhaps we have failed to obey (Luke 11:28; John 14:15).

Cautions

Listening prayer is no substitute for deep, consistent Bible study. We must never isolate a few Scripture verses from the remainder of God's message, or we can easily be deceived.

Neither must we rely on others to get the word of the Lord for us. The Old Testament, 1 Kings 13, tells a sad story of a man of God who allowed another prophet to "amend" God's clear direction to him, and he was killed by a lion on his way home.

When we cannot hear Him

God can and will speak to us, but we must not automatically expect a response from God every time we bow our heads. **God is not a push-button deity**. Sometimes the heavens are like brass, and we cannot understand why. But Jesus taught to ask and keep on asking, to seek and keep on seeking, to knock and keep on knocking (Matthew 7:7). My own times of searching have drawn me out of my self-centeredness into new comprehensions of God.

On one fourteen-hour automobile trip to Oklahoma, I spent the time in earnest prayer, first for one of my children, then for myself, and finally, that He would simply reveal Himself to me. When I truly sought His presence, I began to receive the answers I needed. This kind of prayer stretches and matures our faith.

Never underestimate God. He is a wise, all-loving Father, Healer, Comforter, Judge, capable of fierce anger, yet quick to forgive repentant hearts. I love to call Him the Great Untangler, for He knows what I need, and He alone can unravel the snarls of my damaged emotions, my pride, and my confusion. His is the perfect love—tough, challenging love. He wants me to reach above and beyond my own limits, upward to a childlike faith in Him, and outward to a hurting world.

Why journal?

The following benefits of a prayer journal are gleaned from my own experience and numerous other Christians':

◊ Writing our prayers down clarifies them. Writing slows our mind and helps us identify our own deepest desires.

◊ While we are to pray without ceasing (1 Thessalonians 5:16-18), and can pray no matter what we are doing—driving, cooking, cleaning, ironing, etc.—writing our prayers helps us focus.

◊ Previously unrecognized fears, concerns, and sinful attitudes will often surface so that we can bring them to God.

◊ God can tell us exactly what He wants us to know. When we go back and read His words again, we feel great awe. The insight and wisdom He gives us is far above our own.

◊ We have a written document to share with Christian friends as a means of testing every spirit (1 John 4:1).

◊ We have a written record that helps us trace problems in hearing God. If we have failed to obey Him at some point, His voice may fade. Sheep move away from the Shepherd through lack of obedience.

◊ The journal is a priceless source of comfort as we see how God has answered prayer.

A paradigm shift

Over time, as we practice this simple daily discipline, our outlook will change. He gently changes our perspectives. He opens our eyes to see past dirty windows to the beauty that surrounds us. The aggravations of everyday life fade as He teaches us to be more sensitive to the needs of others.

One Christmas when our two children were small and our finances were slim, we managed to buy them their dream gifts—shiny new bicycles. A few toys were displayed under our tiny tree, but the bikes had to be propped against another wall. Their first reaction on Christmas morning was one of disappointment. "Santa didn't bring us very much." Gently cupping their faces, we turned them around so they could to see the real presents. Gasping with delight, they joyously raced to claim their gifts.

God does this for us, exchanging our negative mindsets for joy as we see the wonder of His love.

Recognizing God's Voice

Several different voices run through our thoughts all the time, and we must distinguish between God's words, our own self-talk, and that of Satan. (An entire chapter is devoted to this subject later in this book.) We must guard against the enemy's subtle deceptions that gradually pull us off track.

We hear what's important to us. I have been blessed with the gift of sound sleep and am seldom wakened by even violent thunderstorms. After a night of crashing thunder and lightning, my family is often amused at my surprise. "Oh, did it rain last night?" But when my children were infants, their slightest whimper brought me instantly awake. Because I cared so much, my ears were attuned to their voices.

On the other hand, it's a mystery to most men why women don't hear little mechanical noises. My husband could diagnose my automobile's engine by listening to it run a few moments. I didn't even know there was a problem.

In a similar way, learning to hear the Master's voice is a matter of, first of all, our heart's priorities. Our ears will be opened to what is important. Then we need to discipline ourselves to make time daily to meet with Him.

He promises good gifts to those who love Him. All we need do is ask. Jesus said, "Which of you, if his son asks for bread, will give him a stone? Or if he asks for a fish, will give him a snake? If you, then, though you are evil, know how to give good gifts to your children, how much more will your Father in heaven give good gifts to those who ask him!" (Matthew 7:11, NIV)

What better gift than to have His voice guiding, comforting, instructing, and expressing His love to us every day?

Still, we can be deceived. Our own desires scream at us and pull us away from His leading. From small decisions to life-changing ones, we can make very bad choices to satisfy our own wants. Chocolate chip cookies "call our name." A job across country entices us with visions of money and success. We want marriage and blind ourselves to the other person's obvious faults.

When we find the beds we've made ourselves uncomfortable, we cry out, "God, why did You let me make this mistake?" Filled with regret, we see our own clay feet and realize that, in ourselves, we are nothing. **Only in Jesus are our lives worthwhile.**

Satan's voice is destructive, denying God. It also denies

human worth, ours or others'. He is a liar, a deceiver, and an accuser. He tricks us into sin and then mocks our distress. He crouches at the door of our hearts, wanting to have us. But God says we can and must master this voice (Genesis 4:7).

Our defense against both self-talk and Satan's voice is this: seek God with all our hearts (Jeremiah 29:13). He promises that we will find Him. He will walk beside us, and He will talk with us. Whether we turn to the right or to the left, our ears will hear a voice behind us, saying, "This is the way; walk in it" (Isaiah 30:21).

Is listening prayer scriptural?

In the Bible, the words "obey" and "listen" are synonymous.[4] In both Hebrew and Greek, "obey me," and "listen to me" are the same.

The Bible is full of Scriptures indicating that God's greatest pleasure is in walking and talking with His children. "My sheep listen to my voice," Jesus said (John 10:27).

Those who have watched sheep tell us that a good shepherd leads them. He never drives them. They are the only animal which cannot be herded. Several flocks may be intermingled, but when it comes time to separate, the sheep follow their own shepherd as he leads them out, talking, singing, or whistling. They know his voice.

Every evening, he builds a small enclosure and calls the sheep—one by one—by name to come to him. As they enter, he examines them carefully for ticks or cuts, pulls the burrs from their fleece, and pours healing oil over any injuries, all the while talking to them. To him, each one is unique, and he knows them by name. He cares for them and provides everything they need. But their greatest need is to hear his voice.

In turn, the Lord wants our company. He traveled several miles across the Sea of Galilee just for the companionship of the ordinary fishermen He called friends. Think of it—the God of

Creation wanted to join them in their smelly boat (John 6:16-21). He lived and died to break the barrier separating us from the personal relationship that God intended for His children.

Dialogue with God is the natural order, as evidenced by the stories of Adam, Eve, Cain, Enoch, Noah, Abraham, David, and others. Both Job and Habakkuk dared to question God, and they were overcome with awe by the power and love in His reply. Elijah was a man just like us, not super-spiritual. Yet He listened to God, obeyed, and marvelous things happened (James 5:17-18).

Jesus said, "I only do what I see the Father doing" (John 5:19). Likewise, I believe He only spoke what He heard the Father speaking. His great invitation—the very purpose of His life and death—is for us to also come into the presence of God, to have that same intimate, personal relationship with the Almighty.

Over the centuries, much of our spiritual inheritance became lost in the Dark Ages, obscured by superstition and paganism. The Reformation restored the power of the Scriptures but left out personal communication with God. This is like a bird trying to fly with one wing. He intends us to have two wings:

⋄   His Word, illuminated in our hearts and minds; and

⋄   A close personal relationship—an ongoing dialogue—with Him.

Our Heavenly Father wants us to soar like eagles, spreading wide both wings to rise far above the mundane cares of our world.

CHAPTER 2

How to Begin

WRITE THIS DOWN, FOR THESE WORDS ARE TRUSTWORTHY AND TRUE.
~ REVELATION 21:5

◊ Bring your Bible, a pen, and a journal with you to your prayer time. Personally, I like to use a spiral notebook the same size as my Bible, because I like the way this fits on my bookshelf. (However, my friends tell me I am a bit compulsive about details—I alphabetize the spices in my kitchen cabinets). If you're not a fellow neatnik and the appearance of your bookshelf doesn't bother you, don't let it matter. Whatever size journal works for you, works.

◊ Plan on spending time alone in a quiet, secluded place to listen. Many people find early morning the best and set their alarm clocks a half-hour early. You might take care of some morning tasks before going to bed in order to have adequate time for prayer the next morning. Or if you prefer evenings, set aside time them. Small sacrifices bring glory to our Lord.

◊ Come into His presence with an expectant heart. You may want to listen to songs that lift your spirit. Many mornings, the Lord wakes me with the melody of an old hymn I have not heard in years. As the music fills my heart, I know that He is singing the words to me—a special love song from Jesus (Zephaniah 3:17).

◊ Try to quiet your mind. Move your perceptions from your head into your heart. Remember, God is spirit, and we who worship Him must worship Him in spirit and in truth (John 4:24).

◊ Search your heart and confess any sin you find there. He will not speak to us if our hearts are not pure (Psalm 66:18).

◊ Pray, "Come, Holy Spirit," and wait until you sense His presence. He is gentle and sensitive, like a dove.

◊ Ask what Scripture He would show you, and read carefully and reverently. You may notice familiar passages having new meaning. This illumination comes only by the Holy Spirit and is one of the most awesome experiences of the Christian life.

◊ Write, "Father, show me how to hear Your voice. Shut off my mind and its busy thoughts. What do You want me to know?"

◊ After a few moments of stillness, write down the words that come to your mind, using quotation marks and first person. (For example, "I have been with you through all the hard times of your life.")

◊ Don't edit what you feel God is saying. If you go back and read what you have written, you can easily tell if the words are your thoughts or from God. You will probably be surprised at the love that is expressed--love that is not of your own imagining. You will have a sense of great peace that is not your own. You will also realize that He uses different words or ways of speaking than you do.

◊ If you have any doubt, write, "Father, is this from You, or my own thoughts?" Then write His reply.

◊ Write this prayer, "Father, what helps me hear Your

voice?" Then write down whatever words come to you.

◊ Next, write this prayer, "What hinders me from hearing Your voice?" Write down what you feel He is telling you.

◊ Don't always say, "What do You want me to *do*?" Pray instead, "Lord, what do You want me to *know*?"

Where to pray

Your "prayer closet" is simply a private place where you can be alone and shut out the sounds and the cares of the world. Dr. Ralph Neighbour Jr. refers to this as "The Listening Room,"[1] and places great emphasis on its being the most important part of a Christian's day. "It is mandatory," he insists.

Some people take the words of Jesus literally, sitting in a darkened broom closet. However, in Jesus's day, houses did not have these small extra rooms for storage, and that probably is not what He meant. "But when you pray, go into your [most] private room and, closing the door, pray to your Father" (Matthew 6:6, AMP).

Use your bedroom, the kitchen table, a desk in the den, your office—wherever you can give the Lord your undivided attention. Shut the door, if possible. The more privacy I give myself, the more I feel His awesome presence.

Jesus gave us the example of going off by Himself into the wilderness or up on the mountain to commune with His Heavenly Father.

You can bring this same inner "closet" to group settings. In the old Quaker worship services, people sat together in expectant silence, disciplining their minds and emotions to stillness. They called this "centering down."

Whether it is in the presence of others who respect your need to draw into yourself, or alone in your own special prayer room, this "centering down" is needed. After a few moments, you will feel your thoughts slowing, your emotions calming, and your spirit rise. You will feel that you are completely alone with your Father. It is in this state of spiritual readiness that you can truly pray.

What To read

God showed me years ago that every page of the Bible is a love letter from Him to me. With the Holy Spirit's guidance, I can always find in its pages a special message. I read until the words either seem to leap off the page or my eyes keep returning to one particular verse. Then I write those at the top of my journal page for that day, letting their meaning sink deep into my spirit.

Reading the Gospels, personalizing every command of Jesus, can be a great discipline to aid in developing a personal relationship with Christ. I always encourage new Bible-readers to start with the Gospel of John and then Saint Paul's Epistle to the Ephesians. Many people think they should start at the beginning and read straight through. After the stories in Genesis and Exodus, they get bogged down and discouraged in Leviticus. Though every detail of the Tabernacle is a foreshadowing of Christ and therefore valuable for study, it's my belief that new Christians should undertake this sometime later with a good mentor.

Proverbs has thirty-one chapters, so you can match each one to the particular day of the month. This book, mostly written by Solomon to his sons, is a wonderful way to teach young people. When my son was first saved, he began reading Proverbs in the *Living Bible* and was amazed. "I never knew all that was in the Bible, Mom!"

The Psalms make great devotional reading. Most are a collection of written prayers that begin with the psalmist's complaints and end with God's beautiful answer.

Again, devotions are not a substitute for ongoing in-depth Bible study, an extremely important part of our Christian walk that must not be neglected.

What to write

Write as if you were speaking to someone who knows all about you. He does. Be yourself and be honest. We are to come to God in truth, from the depths of our being. He will not tolerate "snow jobs." Neither do His beloved children need prayer "formulas." He wants us to be ourselves, totally real, devoid of all pretenses before Him.

One morning I began my prayer time with words of praise that had not come from my heart, and He interrupted my eloquent phrases. *"Joanne, what are you trying to hide?"*

Write down any questions that come to your mind regarding the Scripture, and try to determine why He has impressed those particular words upon your heart. Ask, "What do You want me to know, Lord?" Wait a few moments until you become aware of His Spirit rising within you.

Then, on a separate line, enclosed in quotation marks, write whatever words come to you. Use first person, "I" being God. (Example: *"Beloved, focus upon Me—My words, My compassion, and My beauty—and you will be drawn into the Tree of Life."*) Continue writing in this way until you feel you have His complete message.

If you do not understand, on another line, write, "What do you mean by this, Lord?"

Keep asking, "Is this You, Lord?" Pray that Satan will not interfere or bring confusion or wrong direction. Sometimes you might want to share the message with Christian brothers and sisters and ask if they, too, believe that it is from God.

It may be helpful to precede each line with an initial, as "J" for Jesus and your own initial for yourself. Some of my friends use different colored pens, with red ink to identify God's words. My personal method is to use a bullet mark for my words and an arrow for His. For example:

•   Lord Jesus, where am I failing to obey You?

→ *"Dearest daughter, it is not in the minutiae of the day*

that you so carefully and diligently work that you fail to obey. Rather, it is in not proclaiming Me more clearly. Do not cloud or water down My words."

This is the pattern I have followed throughout much of this book—bullets to identify my voice in my journaling, and arrows to identify His. It is my prayer that God will make this clear to you, so that nothing will be confusing. He is not the author of confusion (1 Corinthians 14:33).

Treasure your journal

You will receive renewed blessings by occasionally going back over your prayer journal and using a highlighter to mark messages that have meant most to you. You may want to identify especially important pages with subject headers for ease of sharing.

CHAPTER 3

How Can I Know the Voice is God?

WHETHER YOU TURN TO THE RIGHT OR TO THE LEFT,
YOUR EARS WILL HEAR A VOICE BEHIND YOU, SAYING,
"THIS IS THE WAY, WALK IN IT.
~ ISAIAH 30:21

When we hear from God himself, we have the power to change. As we make listening prayer a part of our daily quiet time, we learn to recognize God's voice more and more. We begin to trust the wisdom and guidance that we receive as being far beyond our own analytical powers.

However, questions may arise: "How do I know that this is not Satan trying to trick me? How do I know if this is not my own mind making up these words?"

We do hear different voices in our thoughts and our spirits, and we need to be able to differentiate between these by becoming aware of the characteristics and motives of each:

◊   God—God the Father; Jesus; and the Holy Spirit

◊   Satan—an evil, destructive spirit

◊   Self-talk—our own voices talking to us

God's voice

God's voice will never contradict the Bible, either in word or in spirit. His message will flow out of, and agree completely with, His sacred Word.

Seldom, if ever, will you hear an audible sound. God's voice speaks to your spirit, not your eardrums. It may be stern, but not angry. It is calm and has authority. It speaks to a deep knowledge within you, so that you will know that you know that you know.

Rebellion will wonderfully disappear as you feel new strength to obey. Imagine a child playing outside. His mother has supper ready and wants him to come in. She may tell one of the other children, "Go tell your brother to come in." The child may not listen to his sibling, but when Mother goes to the door and personally calls him, he obeys—because the mother has authority. It's the same with us. When God speaks, our spirits respond, our stubborn wills recognize His voice, and we submit to His authority.

We recognize that we have spiritual eyes. What listening prayer does is develop our spiritual ears. We sing, "Open our eyes, Lord,"[1] and we understand that our request is for a glimpse of our Savior in a deep spiritual sense. Likewise, when we as Him to open our ears, we would be astounded to hear God's voice in an audible way. Rather, we expect to sense His presence at a deeper level, at the very center of our being, in what we refer to as our "heart."

God's voice will reveal His character—Wonderful Father, Comforter, Giver of good gifts, Almighty, Counselor, Healer, Savior, Provider, Merciful, and All Wise. He is light, and in Him there is no darkness at all (1 John 1:5). He is love—its source, its definition, and its evidence (1 John 4:8, 16).

Someone has counted over eight hundred names of God in the Scripture, every one of them describing another aspect of His goodness. Psalm 103:2-14 gives us a wonderful picture of

Him:

◊ He is the giver of great benefits.

◊ He pardons our iniquities.

◊ He is the healer of disease.

◊ He redeems us when we are in the pit of depression.

◊ He heaps love and compassion on us.

◊ He so satisfies our desires that we feel young again.

◊ He gives justice to the oppressed.

◊ He is compassionate and gracious.

◊ He is slow to anger and abounds in love.

◊ He won't always accuse us or harbor anger toward us.

◊ He doesn't treat us as we deserve or repay us for our iniquities.

◊ His love toward us is as high as the heavens.

◊ He removes our sins from us, as far as the east is from the west.

◊ He has compassion on us, as a good father has for his children.

◊ He knows our human weaknesses and has compassion on us.

◊ He is our Heavenly Father. We can trust in His goodness, power, and love.

God's motive is to build a close friendship with us. He wants us to know Him and trust in His goodness. These Scriptures describe His character and His motive:

◊ "I have come that they may have life, and have it to the full" (John 10:10).

◊ "For I know the plans I have for you," declares the Lord, "plans to prosper you and not to harm you, plans to give you hope and a future. Then you will call upon me and come and pray to me, and I will listen to you. You will seek me and find me when you seek me with all your heart" (Jeremiah 29:11-13).

◊ "I will be a Father to you, and you will be my sons and daughters, says the Lord Almighty" (2 Corinthians 6:18, AMP).

◊ "Since you are precious and honored in my sight, and because I love you, I will give men in exchange for you, and people in exchange for your life. Do not be afraid, for I am with you" (Isaiah 43:4-5, AMP).

◊ "For I am convinced that neither death nor life, neither angels nor demons, neither the present nor the future, nor any powers, neither height nor depth, nor anything else in all creation, will be able to separate us from the love of God that is in Christ Jesus our Lord" (Romans 8:38-39).

When you hear God's voice speaking to your spirit, you will feel confident, empowered, and courageous. It will bear witness with your spirit that it is truth. His voice affects you like a cool mountain stream—calming, yet refreshing and invigorating. He honors your free will. He corrects, but never condemns. He holds out His hands to you like a father toward his fallen child, patiently encouraging you to try again. He is the perfect gentleman, giving you time to think and consider—never pushing or rushing you.

Satan's voice

While God's voice leads us upward, Satan's voice will pull us down.

Satan's character is that of an adversary, destroyer, accuser, and spoiler. He is the father of lies, tempter, and deceiver. Scriptures also call him the evil one, the devourer, a thief, and the accuser of the brethren.

His motive is to destroy us, because we are God's creation. I do not believe he can directly destroy us. Rather, he tempts us to destroy ourselves. From the time we were small children, he whispered in our ears: "No one's watching."

When I taught children's church, I used a rubber toy snake and Gideon New Testament to illustrate this. The "snake" would whisper in the children's ears, "Mama's not watching. She won't see you steal a cookie." They were taught to quote Ephesians 6:1 from memory: "Children, obey your parents in the Lord, for this is right." With each word, they beat the "snake" with their little Bible. They loved it and, hopefully, never forgot it.

As my teaching progressed to junior high and high school, so did my visual aids. Satan's promises became lovely flower-strewn fields of pleasure: "Do your own thing," "watch out for number one," etc. The problem was that underneath the flowerbeds was quicksand that would lead to death and destruction.

Anyone who has been the victim of an addiction knows the power of Satan's lies and the death-trap they lead to.

His **motive** is to destroy our relationship with the Father. As well, he wants to ruin our relationships with other people. He wants to spoil our joy. He wants to keep us from the abundant life Jesus has promised His followers.

Satan's **tactics** are to bring fear, discouragement, and doubt and drag us down or immobilize us so that we are ineffective. He has no direct power over our lives, but he tries to trick us into destroying ourselves. He tries to make us feel uncomfortable about going to God in prayer. He urges us to seek instant gratification, whispering in our ears, "This once won't matter."

He loves to damage relationships. He appeals to our pride and our need for revenge. He points out all the faults and weaknesses of our Christian friends to divide us from them.

Watch out for Satan's words:

◇ "Always"

◇ "Never"

◇ "Things will never change"

◇ "It's too late"

◇ "You don't deserve God's help or His forgiveness"

Satan pushes us to hurry and do something on our own or to give up. He will try to convince us that we ought to be able to handle things ourselves. Then, when things don't work out, he's our accuser, telling us, "It's all your fault! You can't do anything right!" Listening to him will result in destroyed self-esteem and confidence.

Scripture tells us something about him:

◇ "The thief comes only to steal and kill and destroy" (John 10:10, AMP).

◇ "Stay alert! Watch out for your great enemy, the devil. He prowls around like a roaring lion looking for someone to devour" (1 Peter 5:8, NLT).

◇ "Some people are like seed along the path, where the word is sown. As soon as they hear it, Satan comes and takes away the word that was sown in them" (Mark 4:15).

◇ "You belong to your father, the devil, and you want to carry out your father's desire. He was a murderer from the beginning, not holding to the truth, for there is no truth in him. When he lies, he speaks his native language, for he is a liar and the father of lies" (John 8:44).

Satan uses the tactics of a seducer: "No one will know; if you don't do this, someone else will; you're missing something wonderful; etc."

Satan's voice sounds like Las Vegas looks: glittery and garish. You feel a hypnotic pull towards it; you feel a bit mesmerized. There is often a sense that you have lost your will, a feeling that you can't stop what you are doing. This voice tempts you to make quick, rash decisions. [2] He is not unlike a rogue of a man seducing an innocent virgin.

He will make you feel defeated, frustrated, confused, hopeless, and helpless. He will leave you feeling angry and victimized. He will try to persuade you that God's not answering your prayers or is much too slow.

People who have been involved in the New Age movement and/or witchcraft tell us that it is easy to know the difference between God's voice and Satan's. Whereas God's voice is soothing and quieting, the demonic voices sound insistent, demanding, and mesmerizing, and talk all at once. [3]

Resist Satan's lies by using Scripture against him. God tells us to "resist him, and he will flee from you" (James **4:7). It is also important to claim the blood of Jesus.** "And they overcame him because of the blood of the Lamb" (Revelation 12:11, KJV).

Self-Talk

This is what we say to or about ourselves all day long. Some of it is positive. "I am smart, and I can do anything I put my mind to." Sometimes it is critical or negative. "You are so stupid! You never do anything right!" It usually has two themes:

◊ More praise than we need, or

◊ More condemnation than we need.

Much of this comes from our childhood, the voices of our parents, either excessively doting or excessively critical. **God's voice is different than that of our parents.** He is the Perfect Parent, and always communicates His truth to our spirits.

Self-talk speaks from insecurity. It echoes the values and standards of this world, rather than the attitudes and values of God and His Kingdom. Self-talk is driven by our need to be accepted and acceptable.

Negative Input

I can still hear my mother's reprimanding voice. "*Jo-anne! Why did you do that?*" Strong-willed and too adventurous, I tried her limited store of patience. Although she did not mean to make me feel unloved, I came to think of myself as a "terrible child."

Then, when I was twelve or thirteen, I overheard my father say to my mother, "Our gal's gettin' homelier ever' day." What he *meant* was, in his joking way, I was beginning to grow into young womanhood. But those words burned into my tender emotions and persuaded me that the girl I saw in the mirror was, in fact, unattractive and unlovable.

God never makes that mistake. He never calls us "ugly." He may say, "Beloved, you need to comb your hair." We will look to Him and His great love and be radiant (Psalm 34:5). **Unless self-talk is disciplined to listen to God's voice, it will be the voice of your parents, pushing and prodding you.** It will follow what the world says:

◊ "Pull yourself up by your own bootstraps."

◊ "Look out for number one."

◊ "I can do anything I put my mind to."

It takes its values and standards from the world. It claims that your value is based upon what you do or don't do. **You can never measure up to the standards of your own flesh.**

If we listen to critical self-talk, we will feel drained of energy or motivation. We will always be tired, and will be tempted to give up. It makes us dislike ourselves.

A critical spirit

On the other hand, we may elevate ourselves and disparage others, becoming proud and judgmental. We fall into Satan's traps when we allow our self-talk to contain accusations about ourselves or others.

We seem to think we shall somehow become better people if we keep criticizing ourselves or others. We mistakenly believe this to be motivational. It is not. Rather, it makes us focus on ourselves rather than on the Lord. This critical self-talk will divide us from others—either we meet our self-made standards and feel superior to others, or we fail to meet them and feel inferior. **This is not of God.**

The self-talk voice makes us feel demoralized, insecure, and full of self-hate. It drives us to judge ourselves inaccurately, either elevated too high or brought down too low. It sends us into mood swings between trying harder and wanting to give up entirely.

Put the following Scriptures in your arsenal against self-talk:

◇ "Those who are dominated by the sinful nature think about sinful things, but those who are controlled by the Holy Spirit think about things that please the Spirit. So letting your sinful nature control your mind leads to death. But letting the Spirit control your mind leads to life and peace" (Romans 8:5-6, NLT).

◇ "Finally, brothers, whatever is true, whatever is noble, whatever is right, whatever is pure, whatever is lovely, whatever is admirable—if anything is excellent or praiseworthy—think about such things" (Philippians 4:8).

To turn off these thoughts, pray, "Lord, I'm listening to myself. I want to hear Your voice." Do this every few seconds if necessary. If you really are battling self-talk, go to the Bible and read aloud. This will help drown out other thoughts.

Immersing ourselves in God's truths is our best weapon against both Satan's voice and self-talk. Praise and worship music also helps focus our minds on Him instead of ourselves.

Verify with scripture

We need not doubt God's voice. His message will always be in complete harmony with the Bible. We must stay immersed in the Word. We know the Bible is true, and it will confirm and balance the words you have heard and written in your journal.

Beware of anything outside the boundary of biblical revelation. Peter Lord writes in *Hearing God:*

"The Bible contains a record of God and his dealings with man. In it there is a clear revelation of God, his character, his ways, his will, and his commands. God's principles are consistently portrayed and clearly spelled out. We must forgive as we have been forgiven. We must love our enemies and not seek revenge. It is wrong to steal. It is wrong to judge others. The Holy Spirit will never guide us to do things that are outside the boundary lines of biblical revelation, things inconsistent with the character of God, things divergent to his ordained ways, or things inconsistent with His explicit command." [4]

Always begin your prayer time with Scripture, trusting that God has a personal word for you. Read until His message imprints itself upon your heart. Write the verse at the top of your journal page. When you read back over your prayers and His responses, you will almost always find that He has woven a beautiful pattern of unity, and the Scripture verse is exactly what you need.

So long as we stay firmly entrenched in His Word and test every message against the Bible and against the Lordship of Jesus Christ, we can safely practice this prayer technique.

Testing the message

"*Test everything that is said. Hold on to what is good*" (1 Thessalonians 5:21, NLT). The voice we believe to be God's must affirm Jesus Christ as Lord and Savior, crucified, buried, and raised to life for our redemption. The enemy cannot stand the name of Jesus being honored.

Consider share your journal with another committed Christian from time to time, reading it aloud. The person you choose as prayer partner must be sensitive to the Holy Spirit and able to be totally honest with you. If they sense in their spirit that the messages are God-breathed, that is confirmation.

It is very important to stay in relationship with others. **If you isolate, it is easy for you to go off track.**

Other media

You may not be a writer, and you may find your first attempts at journaling difficult. I would encourage you to keep trying. I've known many people who felt they didn't have the necessary skills, yet after a few weeks, their journal entries flowed with beautiful insights. God is a master writer!

When our hearts are attuned to hear God's voice, we will hear Him speak in many ways, according to our individual natures. Although not by any means talented in art, I found that He could speak His love to me with crayons and construction paper. I asked, "Lord, what do You see when You look at me?" and began to draw.

The result was a joyous array of bright red hearts pasted to a sunny yellow background, and the message, "*I delight in you! Sometimes you make me laugh out loud!*" How awesome to know that I bring joy and delight to my Heavenly Father!

Some people hear His words best in music, often letting Him write beautiful songs of praise. Others freely dance before Him as He choreographs their steps.

When my life crumbled around me and fear hid His voice, He used music in a mighty way to penetrate my stormy emotions. My husband was diagnosed with cancer, and all I could do was plead, "Father, where are You?" Soon, an almost-familiar melody, one I had not heard in many years, began running through my mind. Finally able to identify a few words, I ran to the hymnal to find the precious words of comfort that I needed so much, an old hymn by Annie Johnson Flint and Hubert Miller called, "He Giveth More Grace." [5]

> He giveth more grace as our burdens grow greater,
> He sendeth more strength as our labors increase;
> To added afflictions He addeth His mercy,
> To multiplied trials He multiplies peace.
>
> When we have exhausted our store of endurance,
> When our strength has failed ere the day is half done,
> When we reach the end of our hoarded resources
> Our Father's full giving is only begun.
>
> Fear not that thy need shall exceed His provision,
> Our God ever yearns His resources to share;
> Lean hard on the arm everlasting, availing;
> The Father both thee and thy load will upbear.
>
> His love has no limits, His grace has no measure,
> His power no boundary known unto men;
> For out of His infinite riches in Jesus
> He giveth, and giveth, and giveth again.

I typed those words on a card to place in my kitchen window, and they brought peace and hope to me daily during the next difficult months. God's words bring life and are far better than food and drink to our hungry, thirsty hearts. I urge you to pursue your search for His voice with great anticipation and unflagging zeal.

Come to My feast," He beckons. Taste and see for yourself that the Lord is truly good. He yearns to talk with you, and you will find His voice sweeter than honey and more comforting than a mother's kiss.

CHAPTER 4

Hearing God's Voice in Scripture

THE WORDS OF THE LORD ARE FLAWLESS,
LIKE SILVER REFINED IN A CRUCIBLE,
LIKE GOLD PURIFIED SEVEN TIMES.
~ PSALM 12:6

"The first principle in beginning to listen to God is that of taking the holy scriptures into our very spirits and souls by prayerful meditation upon them. His word then 'abides in us'... God's word aflame within."[1]

I cannot stress enough the importance of staying immersed in His Word. If you are not familiar with the Scriptures, I urge you to begin right now reading a chapter or two of the New Testament every day, underlining those passages which speak to your heart. As God's words permeate your mind and spirit, you will begin to see His fingerprints and evidences of His love all around you.

Bible knowledge is not enough

A person can be very well-versed in the Bible, yet have no understanding. Much of my life, I have been an example of this absence of God-given wisdom.

My dad was an oil-well and water-well driller for many years, and our family moved around Kansas following his work. Shortly after I was born, we moved to the small town of Victoria, which at that time had only a Catholic school. Since we were Protestant, my six-year-old brother was excused from the catechism classes on condition that he would be taught religion at home. Dutifully, Mother bought a copy of *Hurlbut's Story of the Bible*[2] and read it to him daily. Shortly afterward, we moved again. His need for special religious training was past, and the book gathered dust on our bookshelf.

When I reached school age and became an avid reader, I found the storybook and made it my own. To a lonely little girl, it was a special treasure, full of wonderful pictures and enchanting tales. I read it over and over, cover to cover, even acting out the stories. Once (unbeknownst to my mother) I tried to resuscitate a dead rabbit after the manner of Elisha raising the Shunammite boy. (It didn't work, but neither did I get sick—surely a miracle itself!)

So I learned all the stories of the Bible—but I still did not know Jesus.

To add to my head knowledge, my fifth-grade teacher, Mrs. Holland, had our class answer roll call by reciting the books of the Bible. One little girl named Donna could make it all the way to Revelation. I could never make it through the Minor Prophets, but I still learned enough to navigate the Bible without index tabs.

Again, I knew the Bible, but still I did not know Jesus.

Baptism at age twelve did not give me a personal relationship with Him, nor did it keep me from falling into rebellion and wrong company later. I was sixteen when, at an old-fashioned revival, I fell on my knees at the altar and repented of my waywardness.

The door to knowing Jesus had just begun to open.

The Evangelistic Chapel, Guymon, pastored by "K" and Mona Kerr, had a strong youth group, and I spent so much time there that my parents became concerned. Finally, they decided to go to the church to see what was going on, and there they, too, were saved. Unless something completely unavoidable interfered, they never missed another Sunday.

Through the ministry of the little church, I learned to have a morning quiet time. Daily, the Scriptures became more and more alive, and I began to see His love on every page. The veil that Saint Paul described as covering unbelieving hearts was being slowly taken away (2 Corinthians 3:16).

Then, an atheist mocked me and sowed seeds of doubt that troubled me for almost twenty years, well hidden beneath layers of outward Christianity. One of my Christian "habits" was a short devotional, using *Bible Pathway*,[3] with my breakfast coffee. One memorable morning, as I finished the Gospel of John, those doubts were wonderfully resolved, and I recognized the Bible as truly God's Word.

Every person travels his or her own path toward this revelation. This is how God revealed it to me: I was a fledgling writer and realized that stories written by man must fit the framework of human experience, either ours or someone else's. I had also owned and operated a small business and knew the importance of delegating responsibility only to the best qualified and most loyal. In the incredible forgiveness Jesus showed Peter—and then giving this lying, denying fisherman His own mantle of leadership—I recognized a story beyond human imagination. Then, a few pages later, at Peter's words, "It was impossible for death to keep its hold on him" (Acts 2:24), something exploded in my heart, and I began to weep. Turning to my bewildered husband, I cried out, "It's true! The Bible really is true!"

I am still growing, ever learning, far from complete understanding. But I have become enthralled by the incredible courage and beauty of Jesus. His Word begins my day and resonates through my mind and heart as I go about my work. This has led into a beautiful relationship with Him through listening prayer.

The power of the Word

I have a friend, Tom Hoke, for whom drugs and alcohol were a way of life as he spent his days looking for a high and not caring for his children or his wife. The sheriff's department in his small town knew of his activities and had laid traps to catch him. It was only a matter of time before he'd be in jail, bereft of friends and family. He even thought of taking his own life. This was, Tom says, the loneliest time of his life.

Then one day he saw a copy of the Living Bible laying on a table in his living room. Idly, he picked it up and began to read. Several times before, he had tried to read the Bible, but it made no sense to him. This time something was different: Every word became a motion picture in his mind. Not only did he understand the words, he saw them taking place.

He had not finished high school and was a slow reader. But over the next several months, as he read from Genesis to Revelation, God delivered him from drugs, alcohol, cigarettes, and abusive language. He stopped cursing his children and began to tell them about Jesus. In fact, he told everyone about Jesus.

He began attending the Evangelical Friends Church and asked if he could share the experience he had with the Lord. Many of the members knew him and testified his new life was nothing short of God's miracle.

Tom went on to become a dedicated church leader, earning the respect and admiration of all who know him as well as that of a city that once wanted to put him behind bars. He started a ministry for disaster victims (Friends' Disaster Service, League City, Texas), coordinating a group of skilled Christian men and women in rebuilding homes for people whose lives are devastated by hurricanes, tornadoes, fires, or floods.

His life and the lives of those around him were incredibly

transformed through the simple act of reading God's Word.

A suggestion for Bible study

It's a shame that our children are denied Bible teaching in school. One hour a week in Sunday school cannot give an understanding of the majestic sweep of this wonderful book which has inspired millions through the ages. As the foundation for every other aspect of learning—history, science, art, etc.—God's Word ties it all together and makes the picture complete.

Few of us can afford to go to Bible college. But now, since the advent of the Internet, we can find good online courses we can take at home. My friend, Ralph Neighbour Jr., has written a great study course called *Cover the Bible*[4] by which, in only five minutes a day for a year, a person can gain an excellent understanding of God's Word.

To really understand the Bible, it is essential to be committed to Jesus as Lord and Savior. When we accept Christ, we receive the promised Holy Spirit, who becomes our guide into truth (John 16:13). One of the mysteries of God is that He reveals Himself only to those who seek Him with all their hearts (Jeremiah 29:13). Jesus could have settled forever the doubts about His resurrection had He shown Himself to the authorities, but it was only to those who loved Him that He revealed Himself.

I'm blessed with an assortment of Bibles, including my mother's King James and several newer translations and paraphrases. In addition, I like to keep a good thesaurus handy to be sure I understand the connotation of unfamiliar words. Another reference book, a bit more expensive, is a Greek-English lexicon, which I find invaluable in understanding the full meaning of passages.

Sadly, many Christians study the Scriptures to defend their personal beliefs against those of another denomination. I am so glad to see these silly arguments and denominational barriers falling to the wayside as we join forces to confront the indifference and paganism that abounds in America. Saint Augustine's words, "In essentials, unity; in non-essentials, diversity; in all things, charity," are more appropriate today than ever.

Non-believers sometimes read the Bible to try to disprove it. Many times this backfires, and the reader realizes he was wrong and the Bible is true.

As an atheist at college, Josh McDowell decided to prepare a paper that would examine the historical evidence of Christianity in order to disprove it, and ended up as one of the foremost defenders of the faith of the twentieth century. [5]

Lee Strobel was another atheist who used his skills as an investigative reporter to disprove Christianity's claims. His conclusion: "Based on the cumulative weight of the evidence, it would require more faith for me to maintain my atheism than to embrace Jesus as being God's unique Son." He has since authored a number of excellent books[6] to answer the skeptics' hard questions.

A young woman in a juvenile detention center told me that, before she became a Christian, she read the Bible all the way through and decided it was just a bunch of lies. Her parents were atheists, so she was undoubtedly preconditioned to that conclusion. Then, when her life fell apart and she faced prison, she found herself praying, "God, if You're there, please help me!" When she opened her heart this tiny crack, she found Jesus. Now she loves the Bible and finds every word illuminated with God's love.

Different Bible Translations

The Bible is the all-time bestselling book in the world, and most American homes have at least one copy. I am by no means a scholar of Bible history, but I have a deep appreciation for those heroes of the faith who have shed their blood to enable

us to have a copy in our own language. I also am in awe of the way God has preserved the Scriptures over the centuries. When the book of Isaiah in today's Bible was compared with the scroll hidden over two thousand years ago, there were only thirteen words that differed, and these did not change the meaning!

There are copies of the New Testament in existence dating back to 150 A.D., which makes the Bible foremost among ancient manuscripts for authenticity. In 384 A.D. Saint Jerome completed the Latin Vulgate version, of which 10,000 manuscript copies exist today. Before the printing press, monks were assigned to make handwritten copies, with a brother counting each letter and each word to insure complete accuracy. Even if a king should walk in the room, they were taught to take no notice. Nothing was to distract them from their sacred duty. A monk who copied hours on end every day, even by candlelight, might finish one copy of the Bible in about ten months.

Today, we have numerous Bible translations available in many languages, and we can trust that great care has been taken to preserve the original meaning. Unfortunately, there are a few on the market that change words or phrases in such a way that the divinity of Christ is questioned. Before purchasing a particular version, it is best to ask a mature Christian whom you trust. **The test of any version of the Bible is if it reveals Jesus as the Son of God, born of a virgin, sinless, crucified for our sins, resurrected on the third day, and ascended into heaven to be Lord of lord and King of kings.**

If these criteria are met, you will hear God speaking to you through its verses. When I first received a Bible as a gift, it was a new translation and I was hesitant to use it. But after a few days, I found myself exulting, "It works!" God spoke to me through its pages.

CHAPTER 5

Hindrances

PUT ON THE FULL ARMOR OF GOD
SO THAT YOU CAN TAKE YOUR STAND
AGAINST THE DEVIL'S SCHEMES.
~ EPHESIANS 6:11

This study would be incomplete without a reminder of the walls of our own making that we need to guard against.

Listening with our mind instead of our spirit

The wonder of Jesus and His lordship cannot be comprehended with the human mind. Rather, this deep knowing comes in our spirit. When Peter recognized Him as Christ, the Son of the living God, Jesus replied, "This was not revealed to you by flesh and blood, but by my Father in heaven" (Matthew 16:17). This knowledge cannot be grasped with our mind, nor can we explain it.

I sometimes conduct ministries to the elderly in a nearby nursing home. One of their favorite stories is about a homeless boy who found a good meal, a warm bath, and a cozy bed by repeating the magic words, "John 3:16." He had no idea what the words meant, but he knew they "sure made a hungry boy full, a dirty boy clean, and a tired boy rest." When the Scripture was explained to him and he gave his heart to Jesus, he said, "John 3:16—I still don't understand it, but it sure makes a difference in a boy's life."

None of us can explain the mystery of the Gospel, but we know it makes all the difference in our lives. Neither can we understand why God would want to speak to us, but we know, and we know that we know, the precious voice that brings direction and protection the moment we turn to Him.

We may not be familiar with His voice, but when we hear it in our spirits, we will recognize it. Our minds will then understand how to apply it.

Busyness

A crowded schedule too easily gets in the way of the time we need to spend alone with the Lord. He knows what we have to do and will calm our minds and help us think with clarity as we ask His guidance in planning the day. Then, hour by hour, task by task, we are conscious of Him working alongside us, helping us find misplaced objects, meet appointments, overcome obstacles, and sweeten relationships. It is so satisfying to work hand in hand with God!

God has gently worked with me on this issue, for I tend to find too much value in my accomplishments. I make too many promises, and then have to work too much to keep them all. When I think of all the tasks and projects I have started, I am dismayed. An old Irish prayer says, "May you be met in Heaven with all the quilts you meant to make on earth." And all the books I meant to write, and the flowers I planned to grow, and...

One morning He told me, *"Filter these through the blessing they will be to others. If you only try to 'finish undone projects' without applying this filter, the work will just be busy-work, time-consuming, 'fill up the empty hours' busyness. I have not called you to that. Look at all your endeavors and see them through My eyes. Let the rest go."*

We miss one of God's richest blessings if we do not put aside special time for listening, being still before Him, and receiving His love. Not only do we need time set aside each day seeking His guidance, but also on occasion several uninterrupted days of basking in His presence will bring great benefit.

When my daughter was laid off from work, she decided to spend two or three days at a rural retreat, praying and seeking God's will for her future. Family and friends had advised her to change her nursing specialty, but she was unsure if that would be God's will for her. She also has a heart for ministry and yearned to spend more time sharing Christ's love.

After many hours of "soaking" in prayer, she heard the Lord say, *"Crystal, you are highly favored and deeply loved."*

This was not the answer she expected, but it thrilled her heart. Sobbing in joy, she fell to her knees. "Could God really say that to me?"

A great peace filled her as He assured her, *"Yes! You are highly favored because you carry my son Jesus deep in your inner being."*

His words mirrored those spoken to Mary by the angel Gabriel in Luke 1:30.

Crystal's response burst from her lips. "I am your servant. I will believe what You say. Thank You for touching me and loving me in my humbled state."

She received a sudden vision of an earthly father placing his fingers under his child's chin and lifting the little one's head to look into his eyes. With great joy, she cried, "Jesus, You are the lifter of my head!"

Noise

Some people can tune out a noisy environment, but most of us need a quiet, solitary place to be able to hear God's voice. It may be necessary to turn off even Christian radio and praise music to truly "be still and know that He is God" (Psalm 46:10). A friend of mine resorted to earplugs to shut out distractions, and he says it made all the difference for him.

Anger and resentment

Emotions can cloud our thinking and, even more so, our spirit. There seems no solution except to determine not to be led by our feelings. It takes enormous self-control to hold our tongues and make no rash statements or actions until reason has resurfaced and the Holy Spirit is again our guide. As God told Cain, "Sin is crouching at your door; it desires to have you, but you must master it" (Genesis 4:6-7, AMP).

When anger surfaces, we can choose to **react,** as Cain did, letting his emotions direct his actions. Or we can **respond,** accepting God's correction and being led into greater maturity and wisdom.

Recently, I felt His stern admonishment. Offended by someone who treated me as if I were not important *(How dare they?)*, I spent a sleepless night nursing my grievance. When I began my morning quiet time, I had every intention of doing a little whining to God. But the Scripture that leaped off the page of my Message Bible was Proverbs 30:10. "Don't blow the whistle on your fellow workers behind their backs. They'll accuse you of being underhanded, and then you'll be the guilty one."

I blushed with shame at these words, remembering how I had criticized another employee in the presence of our supervisor. Then, led to look up the word *underhanded* in my thesaurus, I wrote down the synonyms. Each one condemned me—unethical, unscrupulous, unprincipled, devious, tricky, sneaky, surreptitious, stealthy, covert, evasive, furtive, coning, cunning, and crafty. All I could do was plead for His forgiveness and ask Him to perform spiritual surgery to remove this terrible flaw from my character.

Then I began to write His answer: *"Now that we have*

identified this imperfection in you, what imperfections in others did you want to discuss?"

"N-none, Lord Jesus!" Even my handwriting shook a bit.

He then said, *"Go your way and sin no more. When you tear another down by criticism, you are destroying Me. It is My reputation that you tear at. There is to be none of this in My Body. Rid yourself of all resentment and of all self-seeking. Quit trying to be important. Don't you remember My words, the last shall be first and the first last? Be satisfied that you and your behavior are very important to Me. I have begun a good work in you and will complete it—to be remolded into a beautiful likeness of Me."*

The most difficult part of His instruction was yet to come. *"Confess your faults one to another, and you will be healed."*

When I obeyed and shared this with my supervisor and the other employee, the blessing of His counsel multiplied. I cannot describe the love I felt, knowing that my Heavenly Father cared enough for me to correct me in this fashion.

Talking too much

The wisdom Solomon desired is more accurately translated, "a God-listening heart" (1 Kings 3:9, MSG). When we do most of the talking, we keep ourselves from hearing God's voice. How can we hear if we do not listen? We need to wait quietly and reverently before Him, letting His presence enfold us and His Spirit speak to ours. Give us hearing hearts, Lord!

If you're having trouble hearing God's responses, try making your part of the prayer dialogue short and concise, expressing your questions or needs in one or two sentences. Remember, He already knows all about the problem, much more than you do.

Impatience

We may not be hearing because we are impatient for

His answer. **We cannot hurry God.** Remember, He is omnipotent. His ways are higher than our ways. A delayed answer may be an even more wonderful answer.

We need to allow ourselves time to spend with Him. One morning He said, *"Just sit here awhile. Your work will wait. I have chosen you to be My friend. The words I speak to your heart will be more and more important in the days ahead. Write them on your heart. You are surrounded by the beauty and peace of My creation. Let that beauty and peace permeate within."*

Presumption

We may not hear His answer to our questions because: 1) we are asking the wrong questions; or 2) we think we already know His answer. For years, my questions were, "Lord, is it okay if I do such-and-such?" If He did not immediately stop me or put a wall in front of me, I assumed His answer was yes, which was of course what I wanted to hear. Needless to say, I got in a lot of trouble following this kind of "leading."

I have learned instead to pray, "Father, what do You want me to know?" or "What would please You?" Listen with a yielded heart, for there is a direct link between yielding and hearing.[1]

Fear

We may have many fears as we try to hear God—fear of misunderstanding and making mistakes, fear of His condemnation, fear of His leading, even fear that He will not talk with us. He knows and understands every one of our fears and will gently help us overcome each one. As we draw closer to Him and comprehend His great love for us, these will dissipate. "Perfect love drives out fear" (1 John 4:18).

We may hesitate telling people, "I believe God spoke to me." They might think we are one of those psychopaths who commit heinous crimes after supposedly hearing from God. A little pride and self-interest may have to be sacrificed. God knows our hearts and is the best protector of our reputations.

Actually, it seems as if believers are quickest to take exception to listening prayer. A friend of mine theorized, "Many Christians would rather make a theological doctrine out of their experience of *not* hearing God than risk learning how to listen to Him themselves." [2]

On the other hand, our instincts direct us to put up boundaries when someone tells us, "God told me you should do so-and-so." We usually feel, with good reason, that we are the victims of cheap manipulation. **Others can help us pray for God's guidance, but it is we ourselves who must hear His message to us.**

Failure to obey

In the editorial notes of my *Christian Growth Study Bible,* I found this wonderful "Axhead Principle," based upon the miracle of Elisha causing an iron tool to float (2 Kings 6). The prophet asked first, "Where did it fall? Where did you last see it?"

The loss of an axe amounted to financial disaster in those days. We, too, can lose a valuable tool—our communication with God's voice. "If you seem to have lost your way, go back to the last time you knew the sharp, cutting edge of God's voice. Then obey. The key question is, 'Have you obeyed the last thing God has told you do?' When we obey His last command to us, it's amazing how much clearer His direction for the future becomes." [17]

Impurity

There is no way we can hide impure lives or impure hearts from God. We must confess and turn from any unforgiven sin. "If I had cherished sin in my heart, the Lord would not have listened" (Psalm 66:18).

As we walk and talk with Him daily, more impurity will surface. One morning He told me, *"I am working on the depths of your heart. As those 'blind spots' underneath the surface are removed, those that you see will become more and more visible, even as an iceberg rises higher as that which is beneath becomes less weighty. You work on the visible. I will work on the invisible."*

Self-righteousness

Jesus said the Comforter would convict us of sin, and of righteousness, and of judgment. These words seem puzzling, but I can see that He is doing just that in my life. Not only does He correct me for overt sin, He has also revealed the pride I take in my own "righteousness," and any judgmental attitudes toward others.

Recently, my friend and I were studying Colossians 3:8-11, which instructs us to rid ourselves of anger, rage, malice, slander, filthy language, lying, and prejudice. I scored myself pretty well in having overcome these faults until I came to "prejudice," pre-judging others and having a critical attitude. These are the words He gave me:

"The other sins, as you have noted, are those of youth and young maturity. Prejudice is one that gains a stronger foothold the older you grow. What would a complete lack of prejudice look like?"

I answered, "Looking at every person past their outward appearance or personality, and listening to their hearts." God, help me shed this tendency to put others in a box of my own judgment!

Over and over, my listening prayers have revealed to me my sin of judging others. Once God said to me, *"See how many 'I's the word 'criticism' has?"*

Another friend received this admonition when tempted to judge another: *"You don't have enough information!"* None of us knows another's heart, another's past, or another's struggles. We don't have enough information to correct another person.

My wise pastor and friend, Ralph Neighbour Jr., warns that correcting others makes them feel rejected, whether the judgment is done overtly or covertly. He calls judging an ugly form of manipulation. In my listening prayer, God has often corrected me strongly for this tendency. He never condemns, but He does insist that I change.

Spiritual Pain

When He begins to wash away such sins in our lives, we may experience some emotional discomfort. This stems from the shifting and straightening of what has become a comfortable mindset. Even as a physical exercise program will leave us weary before we begin to realize benefit, this spiritual exercise will stretch us in ways we had not expected. Take this tiredness to Him. As your personal trainer, He will always encourage and strengthen you.

He may peel off scabs of old, unhealed wounds for cleansing. We often don't realize how these affect our reactions and invade our relationships. Listening prayer will help identify and express suppressed feelings, so healing can begin.

When we recognize a hindrance

The very blocks that hinder our prayers may be those that bring us to our knees for His help. For those of us who have asked Jesus to live in our hearts, He quickly nudges us when our behavior or attitudes smack of self-interest or lack of compassion. Unless we stubbornly persist in our sinful ways, we can expect Him to bring us to repentance.

Among the Holy Spirit's mission is to bring conviction (John 16:8. It is very painful—but altogether necessary—to have His mirror held up before us and recognize the mess we have made

of our lives. However, God doesn't leave us miserable with shame and guilt. It is the enemy who accuses us day and night and takes away hope of restoration. **God lifts up our heads, accepting our repentance, forgiving us, and giving us encouragement and new direction.** There is both love and authority in His voice.

CHAPTER 6

Listening Prayer in Relationships

LOVE EACH OTHER AS I HAVE LOVED YOU.
~ JOHN 15:12

No one can study the New Testament and fail to be impressed with how many of its teachings refer to our relationships with others. Not only our friends, but also those we live with and those we work with are supposed to be the recipients of Christ-like love. Too often our human nature gets in the way, and our hasty words create lasting damage. Listening prayer can be a powerful tool in preventing misunderstanding and miscommunication.

First, though, allow God to heal your own heart of all shame, guilt, and self-condemnation. Bask in His love! **We have difficulty loving others when we are hard on ourselves, because we don't begin to comprehend how much God loves us.** I can only explain this by drawing a picture of the cross—the upright beam representing our relationship to God and the crossbeam our relationships with others. If the upright is shaky or askew, the crossbeam will not be right.

Conversely, if our relationship with another is not what it

should be, our relationship with God will be affected.

Listening prayer in marriage

Listening prayer has great potential to resolve disagreements between husband and wife. Once an issue is discussed, each can go to the Lord for His opinion. When their notes are shared, if they are still opposed, they can ask Him for further clarification. Even if they do not get any guidance, they will still find peace and refreshment.

Family relationships

It is rare that a mother and her adult children can live together without tension. Five years ago, when my daughter and I both needed a stable home, I purchased a house for us. While many friends expressed doubt that Crystal and I could be house-mates, God has given us grace to resolve every conflict and weave a beautiful, loving relationship.

"How good and how pleasant it is when God's people live together in harmony," Psalm 133:1 tells us. The Lord expanded on this in my listening prayer: *"Beloved, harmony consists of different notes played together to make a pleasant sound. The notes must not be too close together, for that would cause discordance. Although you live together, you must give each other space."*

He continued, *"Be sensitive to your daughter's emotions and respond with respect and love. Weep with her when she weeps and rejoice when she rejoices. Let your prayers always be for her. This is love."*

He has blessed me far beyond what I could possibly deserve with a loving family of three wonderful children, eleven incredible grandchildren, and three adorable great-grandchildren. Their pictures line my wall and make a great prayer list. I can look at each beloved face and pray for them one by one. Several do not yet have a personal relationship with Jesus, but He has assured me my prayers will yet be answered. I believe it was D. L. Moody who had a list of one hundred people he was praying for. During his lifetime, he saw ninety-six of them come to Christ, and at his funeral the other four became believers.

I wish I could share my prayer journal with each one, but God has not yet given me that freedom. Someday, perhaps that dream will come to pass and will draw us into greater intimacy, not only with God, but also with one another.

Listening prayer and children

Little children can be taught to add to their prayers a few moments of listening for Jesus's answer. Often, parents are amazed when they see His answers to their children's "impossible" prayers. Lost pets come home, baby brothers are born, or the longed-for toy the family cannot afford comes as an unexpected gift.

At Touch Family Church in Houston, Texas, children of elementary age are taught listening prayer by their Sunday school teachers, Gee and Deborah Fung and my daughter, Crystal Markham. The children are divided into groups of four or five and gathered around a candle to wait in reverent silence. After several moments, when it is evident that they have something to say, they are asked what they heard.

In Crystal's group of four children, two said, "I didn't hear anything." Another said, "I saw angels around the church."

The other child, a very shy eight-year-old boy, hesitated to speak, but he tearfully nodded his head when asked. "Did God show you something?" Only after each of the others promised not to laugh was he willing to share. "I saw a light with darkness all around it. Then it grew bigger and bigger, and split into a lot of little lights that went out into the darkness."

Gently, my daughter asked, "What do you think that meant?"

With utmost seriousness, he replied, "The lights are the church and the Christians. We are growing brighter and brighter with Jesus. Then He will send us out into the dark world."

What a great message! He will remember those words forever, and they may change his life and the lives of others. All we need do is teach them and release them—and never, ever laugh.

Friendships

If we ask, the Lord will teach us how to be a better friend. He once spoke to me about my lack of graciousness. *"Begin with this: Make sure you acknowledge each person's presence and affirm their worth. This takes just a moment, but it is the most important moment you can spend."* I realized that I tend to get too quickly down to business when I join a group. The hellos and sincere questions about their lives and families are loving gestures that He does not want me to skip.

He insisted, *"Be interested in others."* He directed me to Philippians 2:4 (NKJV): "Each of you should look not only to your own interests, but also to the interests of others." The Message Bible paraphrases this: "Don't push your way to the front; don't sweet-talk your way to the top."

When I prayed, "Teach me, Father, the gift of real friendship," He answered: *"Listen with your heart, never be guilty of judging, be generous with your time, and be filled with a compassionate heart so that years and months apart do not sever friendship. Be open to the Christ that dwells in others. I am the tie that binds."*

Work relationships

If at all possible, begin your work day with a time of shared listening prayer with fellow employees, coordinating needs and plans for the day. This little daily routine will do more than anything else you can do to eliminate friction and build a sense of teamwork among you.

At Hidden Manna, we ladies who lived and worked there considered ourselves a family that God marvelously put together. However, when any three strong-minded women live and work together, petty conflicts are bound to arise. We found much resolution and great peace in sitting together before the Lord, asking Him to clarify the issues and to help us live together in harmony. We met every weekday morning at 8:00 a.m., expressed concerns, read a selected Scripture, wrote our individual impressions of God's message, shared the insights He had given us, and then prayed aloud with one another. Each of us received slightly different inspiration, yet we saw incredible unity that could only come from the mind of God.

Sometimes our problems were not with one another, but with the work itself. When our old computer crashed, I spent several fruitless days trying to work with a used one that a friend loaned. The other two prayed fervently for me, for they saw that the problem was much bigger than I could handle.

At last, the decision was made to purchase a new one, despite my misgivings at spending so much money. Can you imagine our awe when a check for a new computer arrived that very week from a previously unknown contributor? I cannot help but think the prayers of my teammates were the catalyst that brought God's marvelous answer.

Nevertheless, when I wrote, "Father, thank you so much for the new computer," this was His reply: "*You will find glitches.* [I did.] *Do not be surprised. The work will never be finished. You can never sit back and survey the finished product as a king would survey his kingdom with pride and arrogance. You are My servant, and the work I give you is for your benefit. Thank Me and lean on Me.*"

Sensitive relationships

In all our lives there are people and situations that, despite our best efforts, evoke negative emotions. Ironically, it is often the ones we love the most who bring out this worst side in us. With me, that one is my daughter—the apple of my eye, at once my image and my opposite.

Several years ago, Crystal fell and broke her leg, and I stayed with her a couple of weeks to help her move to a downstairs apartment. Moving has always been difficult for her, and she dealt with her anxiety by oversleeping, ignoring the world around her, and avoiding stress. Bulldozer personality that I am, I arose early, ready to start packing, and became frustrated waiting for her to wake up. Growing more and more irritated, I confronted her rather harshly and hurt her already tender feelings.

I knew that my vented anger was wrong, and I also knew Who held the answer. We agreed to try listening prayer for help in repairing the damage. This is the transcript of my prayer:

• "Well, here I am, Father, as You said to do. I am messed up emotionally. I thought I was doing the right thing by sharing my feelings. All that has done is create a wall."

→ *"What you saw was not an offense against you, which was the way you verbalized it. Rather, you saw her slipping into an old pattern of ignoring the world around her while she escaped into sleep. Explain this to her. Ask forgiveness for jumping on her and acting angry. She does need to listen to Me regarding her sleep."*

• "Then I am not too far off the mark?"

→ *"Your emotions are a warning of a problem. Rather than flaring up, I would rather you would come to Me and pray for wisdom. Your anger and emotional reactions only cloud the real issue. You end up looking like a 'jerk' because you have spent your emotions foolishly."*

After a few more moments of repentance, I sat down beside her and asked if I could read my journal to her. Tearfully, she nodded. As I read, we could almost see the wall between us crumbling and healing taking place.

I had—and still have—a great deal more work to do on my fiery nature. But God promised to take away all my foolish excesses of spirit, of self-centered thinking, of pride, and of unnecessary defenses. In the few months since I began to ask for these changes, those who know me best say they see a new peace in my spirit. I know that I am being renewed and remolded day by day by the Master Potter.

CHAPTER 7

Praying for Guidance

IF ANY OF YOU LACKS WISDOM, HE SHOULD ASK GOD,
WHO GIVES GENEROUSLY TO ALL WITHOUT FINDING FAULT,
AND IT WILL BE GIVEN TO HIM
~ JAMES 1:5

Divine guidance is one of the greatest benefits of listening prayer, but I doubt if it will help anyone win the lottery. God seems to be much, much more interested in changing our hearts than in guiding our decisions. My experience has been that, as day by day He chisels away on my attitudes, I am making better choices. When we get self out of the way, life works much better.

In one of my prayers, I was angry at myself for having forgotten several important things. His response to me was, *"Joanne, beloved daughter, look to Me in all your ways, and I will direct your paths. Seek no glory for yourself. Your mental disc may be 'full,' but if you are connected to Me, you have infinite resources of memory and wisdom."* How refreshing those words were!

Believers who have totally submitted to the lordship of Jesus Christ have His promise to direct them: "In all your ways acknowledge him, and he will make your paths straight" (Proverbs 3:6).

It is most important to search our own hearts for hidden desires and motives when praying for guidance. "When you ask, you do not receive, because you ask with wrong motives, that you may spend what you get on your pleasures" (James 4:3).

Neither can we discern God's will if we are being unduly influenced by others. Never rely on others to get the word of God for you. I Kings 13 tells the tragic story of a man of God who allowed another to be his spiritual ears. **Friends can pray for you and with you, but it is you who must hear from the Lord.**

A word of warning

If the Lord gives us guidance and we fail to act upon it, we will have fallen into rebellion—a sin greater than witchcraft (1 Samuel 15:23). Are we willing to sign a blank check to God?

Asking for wisdom

Loren Cunningham, the founder of Youth with a Mission, tells of spending seven days alone with God, fasting and praying, before making an important decision. Then not only did he feel he had Divine guidance, but also his family, his friends, and subsequent circumstances all confirmed God's message. His vision of waves of young people evangelizing the world seemed impossible until he chose to follow God's direction. Today, Youth with a Mission covers the globe, with thousands of his trainees bringing the lost to Jesus.

Even so, his first Mercy Ship project fell through, and Loren lost the money paid down on the vessel. Recognizing that pride had crept in, he repented, and eventually the vision was reborn. Even for such a totally sold-out Christian, God had to work on his heart before He opened doors.[1]

The best wisdom

Finally, much of the wisdom He seems to give me is to put a check on my tongue, letting Him do His work in other people's lives instead of trying to fix them myself. As He told my friend who was worrying about her teenaged sons, *"You need to say less and pray more."*

For the most part, God takes pretty good care of those I love, but occasionally I feel compelled to help Him out more than I should. It's probably a relief to them for me to pull back and let Him work. A recent journal entry read: "Father, I am concerned for my granddaughter."

He answered, *"Leave her in My hands. Your fears for her do not help. Give her your blessing and let her go."*

Thinking I needed to give Him more instruction, I continued, "Father, I pray you would give her Christian friends, a mission, work to support herself, a good place to live, and—"

God interrupted my list, *"I know what she needs. Just let Me take care of it. You take care of your mission. I will take care of hers."*

CHAPTER 8

Intercessory Prayer

THE PRAYER OF A RIGHTEOUS MAN IS POWERFUL
AND EFFECTIVE.
~ JAMES 5:16

Two long shelves in my hallway hold my most precious prayer list—pictures of my children, grandchildren, and now my little great-grandchildren. Even though some are far away, as I ask God's protection and guidance for each one, I feel very close to them.

Another prayer list begins at the back of my journal. Notes scribbled during church services or home groups about members who are sick, having marital problems, job-hunting, etc. are transferred the next morning to this section of my journal as a daily reminder of urgent needs. After I have completed my listening prayer, I turn to those pages and lift each request listed there to my Heavenly Father. Morning after morning, I find my heart expanding with deeper love and concern. This is the bond that Jesus intended for His Church to experience as we intercede one for another.

What joy it is to receive the report that illnesses and difficulties have yielded to the healing hand of our Master, and to be able to put "PTL" by that request.

Knowing how to intercede

It is important that we listen to God **before** we frame our prayer request. "Listening to the Lord is the first thing, the second thing, and the third thing necessary for successful intercession," writes Richard Foster in *Celebration of Discipline*. "We must hear, know, and obey the will of God before we pray it into the lives of others. The prayer of guidance constantly precedes and surrounds the prayer of faith."[1]

To summarize Mr. Foster, these are several of the points he makes:

◊ When God gives us an inner sense of compassion for another, this is His direction to pray for that person.

◊ Listen for guidance. If we are in communion with God and have His Holy Spirit directing our hearts, His life and power will flow through us.

◊ Do not pray, "If it be Thy will." Jesus did not say this when praying for others, nor did the disciples or apostles. He did not teach indecisive, tentative, half-hoping prayers.

◊ Pray simply, as a little child, with the expectation that change will occur. [2]

Praying for the sick

We need to ask God how He wants us to pray for another. Too often we confuse praying with begging and pleading. Rather, we need to seek the heart of our Heavenly Father. He loves His children and wants to give us all His best gifts.

Intercession makes a difference

We will never know how much difference our prayers have made until we get to heaven. A strong, active woman in our church suffered an aortic aneurysm and stroke and was taken to the hospital in a comatose condition. As her family watched her daily losing ground, one of her sons received a vision of her walking out of the hospital, strong and healthy. A young girl reported a dream of seeing the woman resting her head in Jesus's lap. Despite the doctors' dire warnings that she would be nothing more than a vegetable if she survived, her family and church friends determined to call on God for her recovery. When told they may as well "pull the plug," they refused and asked people around the world to pray for their mother.

Several months later, she is in rehabilitation. Her mind is fully recovered and much of her physical coordination regained. She still has left-sided weakness, but with continued prayer and her strong determination, she will be back in church, praising God not only for her recovery, but also for the unity He brought among members of her family as they joined hands and hearts in prayer.

Praying For our Families

Which of us who have managed to see our children safely grown have not experienced miracle after miracle of God's grace? I think back to my own children's turbulent years, when several times God set off all my inner alarms and sent me racing to rescue them in what could only have been His miraculous intervention.

My daughter was a precious, lively toddler of two when she got into my purse and found some medication. I was busy preparing supper, but when she was quiet a split-second too long, I turned in horror to see her stuffing pills into her mouth with both hands. The doctors at the little clinic nearby gave her an emetic to cause vomiting and assured me she would be fine.

I was a young mother and easily intimidated, but God's warning signals within me sounded, and I insisted on referral to a children's hospital about thirty minutes away. After a wild ambulance ride, we arrived to find the pediatrician waiting at the door. He tucked her under his arm like a football and ran to the emergency room, where he pumped her stomach and kept her overnight for observation. "Five of those pills would have killed her," he explained. She had eaten fourteen!

When our emotions get in God's way

When my older son Michael turned eighteen, he got involved with the drug scene and all its aberrant behavior—violent outbursts, moodiness, inability to hold a job, etc. Only a parent who has experienced the downhill slide of a brilliant child can understand the despair I felt.

Then my pastor from my own teenaged years, "K" Kerr, came to our town to hold a revival. The attendance was terrible, and I grieved that my friend was preaching to empty pews. Taking it upon myself to remedy the situation, I invited everyone I knew. My son and his girlfriend stopped by our shop, and, in a burst of enthusiasm, I asked them to come to the revival. "Well, we might," Michael drawled, leaving unsaid the words, "But don't expect us."

Much to my surprise, they did come, sitting on the back pew where they would not be noticed and could slip out as soon as the service ended. Then, on the last night of the meetings, he came again, this time by himself.

Fervently sending silent pleas for him to respond to the invitation, I heard the Lord's unexpected voice in my ear. *"Don't pray for your son. Your emotions are getting in the way of My work and binding him. Pray instead for yourself."*

When I obeyed, releasing him to the Lord, the miracle happened! Michael stumbled to the altar and gave his heart and life to Christ. Never again did he touch drugs, and he became a sweet, godly young man who amazed everyone.

When our Children are in danger

Four years later, this same son graduated *summa cum laude* with a degree in accounting and landed what he thought was a great job. But soon he found himself in an almost impossible work situation, assigned to a supervisor who seemed determined to break his spirit. As the stress and his frustration increased, he began to get migraines.

One day he called me, asking for advice about his aching head. Something in his voice gave me an all-too-clear picture of his situation. I found a prayer closet (the bathroom) and earnestly prayed, "Lord Jesus, Michael is in deep trouble. If his anger explodes, his entire career is ruined and all his college training goes down the drain. I can't do a thing to help him, but You can. Father, please do something!"

Within the hour, one of the chief supervisors came into the room in which he was working, observed the situation, and had him reassigned to another office!

A friend of mine told of an awesome instance of God's leading. Her daughter, who lived in a nearby town, fell into deep suicidal depression. She relates: "I don't know how I knew, but one evening I suddenly became aware that her life was in danger. I must have driven ninety miles an hour—while angels cleared the highway—to her apartment complex and persuaded the apartment manager to open the door."

Her daughter told her afterward, her voice still shaking with amazement, "I could not believe it! Mom, I had the razor blade pressed to my wrist and was trying to get enough nerve to cut, when I heard you shouting and pounding on my door!"

There are times like these when every prayer and every fiber of our being must be directed toward our children's protection. However, most of the time, our kids benefit more when we get our own spiritual houses in order.

I cannot improve upon Peter Lord's comments on this matter: "Like me, most people asking God for a change in their family situation are seeking guidance in how to help the other member(s) of the family change. I, for example, earnestly prayed for a change in my son, Richard, when he was involved in drugs. But God usually works first in the 'pray-er', the person doing the praying. God dealt with me about my pride before He ever answered my prayer and touched Richard." [3]

Mr. Lord continues, "God is more interested in the development of your character than He is in changing your circumstances.... He knows that when Christ is in charge in you, the circumstances will change you. He may or may not change the circumstances."

For many years, I nursed an old childhood grudge toward my brother. Since we lived far apart, my hostility was not something that should have affected my own family. Then, when I joined a codependent's twelve-step program, I had to work on the relationship between the two of us. After several months of letters, both of us asking and receiving forgiveness, we were marvelously reconciled.

He always said that the fall of the Berlin Wall that year was not a greater miracle than that of the wall between us coming down! I can look back and recognize this as a definite turning point for our entire family.

Two years ago, my brother passed away, and I flew to Arizona for his funeral. His precious widow asked me to say a few words at his funeral, and, after praying, I elected to tell this story. Afterward, several people came up to me with tears in their eyes and said, "Because of what you said today, I will go home and make a phone call. There is someone in my family I need to forgive."

Interceding for our nation

I agree with many people who trace the beginning of my country's downward moral spiral to 1968, the year school prayer was outlawed. The prayers of even little children are instrumental in deterring the forces of evil! It is now up to the rest of us to stand firmly in the gap created by that Supreme

Court decision.

The Bible directs us to pray for our national leaders, regardless of our political leanings. We also must pray for an end to terrorism in the world and for the protection and safety of our troops and for their families back home.

Above all, pray for your nation's families, that the hearts of the fathers would turn to their children, and the hearts of the children to their fathers (Malachi 4:6). Too many children are being raised in abusive homes, too many are joining gangs for the attention they don't receive at home, and too many of these children have babies themselves. Satan has enslaved our young people with his drugs, alcohol, and street life. Many infants are born already addicted to cocaine. The world is rotting from within, and only God can change the destructive course we are on.

Pray as we watch the news

My friend Kathy Ide writes of the days following September 11, 2001, when, as the tragic events of that day unfolded, she found herself glued to the television. She seemed to develop an obsessive compulsion to see the latest news. Watching it morning, noon, and night, she was ready to grab the phone and call friends and loved ones if something happened they might have missed.

One day, she relates, while watching another late-breaking update, it occurred to her how wonderful it would be to have that same obsession about spending time with the Lord. "Not that it isn't important to find out if CNN has anything new," she said, "but shouldn't it be even more important to make sure I don't miss anything God might have to say to me?" How blessed her friends and loved ones would be, she thought, if she called them immediately every time she received His wisdom or insight.

At that moment, Kathy made herself a promise. Whenever she felt the urge to pick up the remote and turn on the news, she would pray. She prayed for our country, for the president and his advisors, and for those who planned evil against the United States and other peace-loving countries. She even prayed for Osama bin Laden and for those who had fallen prey to the lies he perpetrated.

She still watched the news, but only after she had prayed, and only long enough to see if anything major had occurred. Then she turned the television off and prayed some more before going back to her duties. This self-imposed regimen brought her new peace, because her focus was on the God of the universe, who rules over all. [4]

Praying for our world

There is so much suffering in our own nation, so why should we care for people in other countries? It is easy to develop callused hearts because of the constant bombardment of bad news in the papers and on television. Can we learn to stop and pray for those people as individuals whom God created and sent His Son to die for? We must also pray for more full-time missionaries to labor in this great harvest field, opening hearts and minds to His transforming Gospel. Pray even for the terrorists, remembering that nothing is impossible with God (Luke 1:37).

It's during such chaotic times as the world is experiencing today that God brings His mightiest changes. When the world was reeling under the iron fist of Rome, He sent His Son, and from that tiny manger came the message that changed the world. Even as the Roman armies and their roads inadvertently helped spread the Gospel, so the global wars of today and the Internet will be God's instruments in fulfilling His mighty purpose.

CHAPTER 9

Praying for Material Things

BUT SEEK FIRST HIS KINGDOM AND HIS RIGHTEOUSNESS,
AND ALL THESE THINGS WILL BE GIVEN TO YOU AS WELL.
~ MATTHEW 6:33

Our Heavenly Father does not seem to be as interested in giving us the things we pray for as He is in reshaping our character. When I first began practicing listening prayer, I received this message one morning: *"Joanne, I am NOT your magician!"*

Several years ago, my friend Louise was trying to sell her farm (later Hidden Manna Christian Retreat Center), and she begged the Lord to bring a buyer. Months went by while it fell into neglect and property taxes accumulated. Her prayers took on a tone of desperation, pleading for relief. She admits that she became almost irritated when there was no response.

One day, she heard the Lord say, quite clearly, *"Louise, I don't give a flip whether you sell the farm or not. What I do care about is your attitude!"* At that time, she could never have imagined the miracle of the retreat center and its ministry. When He says no, He often has something much better in mind.

When God looks at our hearts, if what He sees does not please Him, He zeroes in on those things—jealousy, pride, anger, discontent. When our prayers are, "Father, what do You want me to know?" and we listen with our spiritual ears, He will point out these things to us. He knows what we need. The question is, are we seeking His righteousness?

A number of years ago, when my husband and I owned a marine supply, I made great effort to collect a large sum of money owed to our business. My best efforts were fruitless, and I was frustrated with my helplessness. The Lord gave me this message: *"When you go to heaven, you will not be asked to account for every penny you did not collect. Neither must you answer to Me for every dollar you did not earn or save. But I will hold you accountable for secret pride and for judgment of others. That is not of me."*

Suddenly, the money no longer seemed important, and with a peaceful heart I filed the bill in the "written off" folder. Several weeks later, another debtor—one that I never expected to hear from again—walked in and paid off a years-old account.

The point seems to be that when we pray, we need always to ask, "Father, what do You want to say to me?" Then be still and listen. He will show us our real needs. He will take care of our material needs in His own way.

When the checkbook is dangerously low

At Hidden Manna, we faced this quite often, for ours was a ministry on a shoestring. Many months we held our breath as air conditioners quit, hot water heaters leaked, or the tractor went on strike. Somehow, some way, God always provided—not an excess, but enough.

When expenses mounted, we prayed. When our bookings dwindled, we prayed. God worked His wonders in many ways, bringing volunteers to help us, a check from an old friend, donated equipment, and last-minute reservations to fill our calendar. As an organization, we learned to trust Jesus to provide for our every need.

God's amazing doors

When Louise reached her seventy-fifth birthday (and I was not far behind), she felt the Lord would have her pursue other visions and put the valuable Hidden Manna property up for sale. Neither of us expected a buyer for many months.

When and if it sold, I idly dreamed of purchasing a house for my daughter and me. A picture came to mind of a three-bedroom brick house on a quiet street with a small yard, nestled among tall trees—a real home for both of us.

The unexpected happened when my daughter's landlord failed to pay the mortgage, and the bank foreclosed on her rented house. Completely unaware of God's fingerprints, I hurried to The Woodlands and helped her move to a temporary room with her married daughter. While there, I reluctantly agreed to look at a house for sale.

Room after room filled me with amazement. It was almost exactly the one in my vision! Two hours later, I wrote a check to the realtor for the deposit.

My head still spinning, I returned to Hidden Manna to confess what I had done and warn I would soon move. Since we had several big retreats scheduled, I promised, "I won't leave until July thirty-first."

Within two weeks, Louise received a lucrative cash offer for the "unsellable" retreat center. The date of transfer: July 31.

Stewardship

Even though my needs are wonderfully provided for, God has impressed upon me the importance of good stewardship of my income. I struggled with knowing where to draw the line on helping my own family, being either too generous or too stingy. Many, many couples are in trouble because of financial pressures. About a year ago, I decided to take the Crown Financial Ministries budget counseling course, mostly for myself, but also in hopes of helping members of my family and others. This is the course developed by Larry Burkett and Howard Dayton to teach God's financial principles.

What the Scripture Crown encourages its students to write upon their hearts is this: "Yours, LORD, is the greatness and the power and the glory and the majesty and the splendor, for everything in heaven and earth is Yours. Yours, Lord, is the kingdom; You are exalted as head over all" (1 Chronicles 29:11). When we recognize that God is the owner of the earth and everything therein, our attitudes about our money and possessions have to change. We are simply stewards—managers—of whatever He places in our care.

My nation is in great jeopardy because of consumer overspending. In 2004, it was estimated that the average American household owed over $18,000 in credit card and car loan debt, not including the mortgage on their home. Balances on credit cards alone averaged $12,000 per household. [1]

Some of our consumer debt can be attributed to the loss of jobs and the downturn in the economy over the past few years. Even more at fault are our undisciplined lifestyles and lack of saving for unforeseen emergencies. Medical costs have soared, pushing many people over the edge financially. Students are using credit cards to pay for their education. The elderly are finding their Social Security income far less than adequate to pay for food, utilities, and health care. Bankruptcies are at an all-time high, as are foreclosures and car repossessions.

Yet the Bible says to owe no man. "Let no debt remain outstanding, except the continuing debt to love one another" (Romans 13:8).

We give up our God-intended freedom when we allow ourselves to become bound by debt. "The rich rule over the poor, and the borrower is servant to the lender" (Proverbs 22:7). In most households, the wife must work, and sometimes the husband holds down two jobs in order to meet expenses. They have no freedom left.

Crown Financial Ministries is addressing a great need, by helping Christians break the slavery of debt and be free to serve the Lord. Volunteers of this organization give seminars in churches and offer personal budget counseling at no charge whatsoever. They can be contacted at their website, www. crown.org.

Debt elimination

To get out of the trap of financial slavery, we need to allow no more debt. It may be necessary to perform "plastic surgery," cutting up credit cards and closing those accounts.

Pray about eliminating debt, asking for the Lord's help and guidance. Every month, send a few extra few dollars toward the bill with the highest interest. Once that one is paid, apply the payment to the next debt, and so on. By this method, Crown teaches, the average family can become debt-free in three years or less.

Develop a good balanced budget, based upon present income without counting overtime or bonuses. When extra money comes in, use it to apply to debt reduction. The first step in budgeting is to keep a 30-day diary of every dollar spent, which will reveal the "leaks" that must be controlled and any regular expenses that can be discontinued.

It's not easy, but it works. By following these financial principles, I have been able to pay off the mortgage on the house I purchased for my daughter and me in a little over four years.

Tithing

I am a strong believer in tithing, although I don't believe in the "prosperity gospel" that teaches an automatic return for every dollar given. I can, however, relate my own experience of long-term, solid blessings. God not only provided for us, but He also blessed family relationships.

In my late thirties, a single mom with a teenaged daughter at home, I began to feel that I should tithe. However, I also had a car insurance premium due on the fifteenth. I called my pastor, who said, "Joanne, I don't believe the Lord wants you to be without car insurance." Somehow, I had peace, knowing that the matter was in God's hands. When payday came and I had paid all my bills, including the insurance, there was enough money left over to tithe. God had provided!

So I began to tithe regularly, and when I remarried, I asked my new husband Tommy if we could continue.

"Well," he said, "I've always heard that you could live better on ninety percent than on one hundred percent."

So we tithed, mostly on my wages, since I continued working at a nearby hospital for several months. His business was in such poor shape that he seldom could bring anything home. If an accountant had prepared a balance sheet, the boatyard would have been entirely in the red.

Finally I was able to quit the hospital job and begin working with him as Girl Friday in the tiny building that housed a shelf for a desk, a drawer of overdue accounts, and disorganized boxes and barrels of merchandise needed for boat repair. He had two employees, who decided I would also keep a pot of soup ready for lunch. With more hope than common sense, I designed a logo and christened the business, "Hillman Marine."

We determined that we would follow God's Word by paying our employees first, our suppliers next, and, if there was anything left, ourselves. We always gave ten percent of this take-home pay to God's work.

Fast forward almost fifteen years, to the meeting called by his executor after my husband's death. Facing his four sons and me with a sheaf of accounting papers, Mr. Marin said, "I have never seen such a sound small business."

I take some credit for the turnaround, for I worked alongside my husband many hours. Mostly I credit God, who gave us a heart to work together and smoothed rough areas so there was no dissension or competition between us. God molded our efforts into a "synergy"—the outcome much greater than the sum of the hours and effort we two put into the business.

As a sad postscript, I must add that a few years after his

death, I married again. That husband agreed to tithe for a while, but finally told me, "I want to quit giving so much. I don't believe in it." I felt I had to submit to his wishes, so we cut our giving to a mere twenty-five dollars a month. Looking back, I can almost date the dissolution of the marriage from that decision.

CHAPTER 10

Overcoming Anxiety

DO NOT BE ANXIOUS ABOUT ANYTHING,
BUT IN EVERY SITUATION, BY PRAYER AND PETITION,
WITH THANKSGIVING, PRESENT YOUR REQUESTS TO GOD.
AND THE PEACE OF GOD, WHICH TRANSCENDS ALL UNDERSTANDING,
WILL GUARD YOUR HEARTS AND YOUR MINDS IN CHRIST JESUS.
~ PHILIPPIANS 4:6-7

Saint Paul penned this "letter of joy" from the confines of a Roman prison, writing to a small group of believers who were facing intense persecution and suffering. All who profess the lordship of Christ, he insisted, can have joy and peace regardless of circumstances.

Contrast those early Christians' lives with our generation, spoiled by comfort and ease the world has never before known. Yet most of us live in a constant state of anxiety. In 1983 *Time* ran an article citing stress as America's number one health problem. [1] Two decades later, despite millions of dollars spent on gadgets, pills, and leisure, worry continues to ruin our health and our relationships.

I am not speaking of the acute distress we feel when a loved one is dying or in extreme danger. At those times, we pray almost constantly for God's intervention. Neither am I referring to responsibilities that demand our effort—bills to pay, gardens to weed, meals to cook, tests to study for, or commitments to keep. We would be fools not to give these things our attention.

The anxiety that hinders prayer and steals away peace is different. It's more of a creeping, unidentifiable unease that pours unneeded adrenaline into our systems and gives the feeling we must "do something" about things over which we have no control. Relaxation becomes impossible, and our relationships with others suffer.

It's not the big crises that get me down. With God's help, those I can handle. It's the day-by-day "stuff" of life that numbs my mind and brings out my worst. Like a swarm of pesky gnats, little problems mounting one upon another nibble at my disposition. Solomon speaks of "little foxes that ruin the vineyards" (Song of Songs 2:15), and the vineyard of my Christian peace is definitely at risk. I feel anxious and snappish, and if you were to meet me then, you would decide I was a very unpleasant person. No one likes me when I'm filled with stress, least of all myself.

Listening prayer has been a definite help, when at last I take a few moments and lay my disturbed emotions before God. A recent journal entry read:

• "Father, what is wrong with me? Why am I so tense? What is going on with me emotionally? Please help me find Your peace again."

→ *"Beloved, you are reacting to some new pressures, some of which you have laid upon yourself by your own unrealistic expectations."*

• "Lord Jesus, I don't want to display an angry, defensive attitude or put others on guard."

→ *"Release the annoyances to Me. Don't keep rehashing them in your mind. Your snappishness is a childish reaction to little irritations. What would be a mature response?"*

- "The first step, I think, would be to look over my list of work that needs to   be done and prioritize tasks."

→ *"And?"*

- "Well, if—when—I've offended others, I guess I'll have to ask their forgiveness.... Some physical work will reduce the muscle tension in my back and shoulders. I can clean out our storage shed today. Putting things in order gives me satisfaction and eliminates future annoyances."

→ *"Where does the love of Christ Jesus come into this?"*

Admonished, I hung my head.

- "He said we must love one another. This was His command, not His suggestion."

I looked again at the definition of love in the thirteenth chapter of First Corinthians.

- "Lord Jesus, I have failed in every one of these areas. Impatience, unkindness, rudeness—all of these are reflected in my expression and my heart. That's not the way I want to be. Change me, Lord Jesus!"

→ *"Put your focus back on Me today. In all you do, acknowledge Me."*

I apologized to my friend and then spent the afternoon in good, hard labor, while audiotapes of the The Message New Testament ministered and soothed my spirit. By evening, the tension and ugly feelings were gone.

Worry vs. Faith

I come by worry honestly. My mom was a champion of the art, watching over my brother and me like a determined mother hen guarding her chicks. Our slightest sneeze would send her to the medicine cabinet for some vile-tasting concoction and strong-smelling chest rub. One dose was usually enough to cure us, no doubt from fear of repeat treatments.

Much of her anxiety was due to her inability to meet her own standards. She dreamed of a well-kept house and a lush garden. Life dealt her instead a poorly built home in southwestern Kansas, where she fought a constant battle against insidious dust, drought, and grasshoppers. She also expected me to be a pretty little girl with long curls and ruffles. To her chagrin, I much preferred overalls and playing in the farmyard dirt.

Still, she was determined to keep us clean, well-fed, and healthy. In my first year of school, I brought home a dreadful, contagious disease known as the "itch." Mother was horrified, considering it something only "dirty people" ever had.

No child was ever scrubbed more thoroughly nor doctored more assiduously. She lathered me with a mixture of sulfur and lard and covered my chair and bed with sheets, which she boiled every day along with every stitch of clothing I had worn. Two weeks later, the rash was worse. She took me to the doctor, who took one look and laughed. "You're keeping her too clean, Mrs. Mayfield. Her skin's breaking out from too much soap!"

She also was a self-taught poet. By the time she turned eighty, she had accumulated a drawer full of handwritten inspirational verses and decided to put them in a book. [2] As I typed her manuscripts in preparation for self-publishing, I was astonished to see in her words the same recurring theme. "Faith?" I puzzled. "She's the worst worrier I've ever known!"

Then, as I kept typing and absorbing the words, I realized I wasn't merely reading "Mom's poetry"—I was hearing God! He was giving her these messages of faith, not because she never worried, but rather to give her the comfort she so needed. In turn, her poems shared with others His beautiful peace.

With deep humility and great pride, I want to share the words of the first poem in my mother's book[2]:

FEAR NOT
By Mrs. Frank Mayfield

Sometimes the flame of your courage
seems to flicker and almost die;
You look at the stream of your faith,
and it seems so muddy and dry.
It seems as if there's no path
to guide you through tomorrow
And each demand life makes of you
is only cause for sorrow.
But there ahead is a tiny step,
one step that faith can see,
And with each step your courage grows
and more faith is given thee.
Though we may never, never know
life's hidden mysterious meaning,
We must walk ahead in faith,
upon God's promise leaning.
He has given us His promise.
We need so little more
Than to know, in all life's journey,
our Father goes before.

My own walk with worry

Before I recognized God's leading in her life, I tried very hard not to follow my mother's anxious footsteps. However, a complete lack of worry was not a good thing, for my overconfident and cocky attitude got me in plenty of trouble in school.

Marriage at eighteen and motherhood were great learning processes. Every year, my mom grew much, much smarter! By the time my kids reached their teens, I was well into the worry pattern.

Is there any way a parent can be free of anxiety? Perhaps,

if we've never held an asthmatic baby gasping for breath. Or haven't yet seen our shy little five-year-old get on the bus for her first day of kindergarten. Or if we have never watched a beloved son get on a plane heading for military boot camp. Our children hold our heartstrings as long as we live.

God spoke these comforting words to one of my friends when she was fretting about her small son and daughter: *"They are My children, entrusted to you, but still Mine. I am with them at every turn. I love them more than even you do. Teach them to hear My voice, and I will guide them."*

I believe God has a special place in His heart for parents' prayers. This doesn't mean, however, that we must fret and stew and try to control our kids. They need our prayers. They don't need or want our anxiety.

Listening prayer

When I began prayer journaling, many pages were filled with worry prayers. Then one day, He asked me, *"What can you do about your daughter's problem?"*

I had to answer, "Nothing, Lord. My fretting accomplishes nothing."

He reminded me then of His words in Matthew 18:18. *"Truly I tell you, whatever you bind on earth will be bound in heaven, and whatever you loose on earth will be loosed in heaven."*

His next words were very clear: *"There is a vast difference between worry and prayer. Worry binds. Prayer releases. Worry tries to control. Prayer gives the reins to Me, the One who is truly loving and truly strong. Even as you cannot stop one hair from graying or halt the advance of the clock or calendar, you have no control over your daughter's situation. Leave her in My hands!"*

This was almost bewildering. "Teach me how to pray for my children, Lord Jesus," I begged.

"Pray this way: 'In myself, I can do nothing, Lord, but You can. I ask that You help them, please.' Remember, when you

release them to Me, you can depend on Me."

Those last words rang in my ears and my heart for days. I didn't need to worry—I could depend on God!

The effects of worry

Peter Marshall once prayed, "Forgive us our ulcers, Father—the badges of our unbelief." [3] If we believe His Word, we can trust Him for tomorrow. Like Saint Paul, we will be convinced *"that neither death nor life, neither angels nor demons, neither the present nor the future, nor any powers, neither height nor depth, nor anything else in all creation, will be able to separate us from the love of God that is in Christ Jesus our Lord"* (Romans 8:38-39).

Anxiety elevates our blood pressure and gives rise to muscle tension, headaches, and back pain. It can trigger an increase in stomach acid leading to ulcers, colitis, or heartburn. Some people break out in hives. It can aggravate asthma. Chronic worry may even compromise our immune system and make us more vulnerable to bacteria and viruses—even cancer, researchers believe.

The word *worry* comes from an Old English verb, *wyrgan*, meaning to strangle, choke, or tear at the throat with the teeth. When we are in anxiety's grip, we may become so immobilized that we cannot see the solution. Faith tells us, "God will make a way," but in the stranglehold of worry, we can see nothing except the problem.

Corrie Ten Boom, survivor of a Nazi death camp, left this jewel of wisdom: "Worry does not empty tomorrow of its sorrow; it empties today of its strength."

Let go and let God

When a little boy's favorite toy broke, he took it to his father. "Fix it for me, please!"

The father worked on it a few minutes, and then the child snatched it out of his hand. Again and again this happened, and finally the boy was crying in his disappointment. "Why didn't you fix it, Daddy?"

His father gently replied, "Son, I tried, but you kept taking it away from me."

To overcome anxiety, we have to learn how to give our worries to our Heavenly Father and then—the hardest part— leave them in His capable hands.

CHAPTER 11

Overcoming Pride

MY SACRIFICE, O GOD, IS A BROKEN SPIRIT;
A BROKEN AND CONTRITE HEART,
YOU, GOD, WILL NOT DESPISE.
~ PSALM 51:17

God is quick to point out one of the attitudes most hateful in His eyes, that of pride. A healthy pride in our accomplishments or in our beautiful children can grow into arrogance that elevates us above others. He has shown me, and continues to show me, the many ways I deceive myself with hidden pride.

Pride in our lack of pride

Pride is one of those insidious things that creep in on a person's blind side when we're attending to something else. We can even be proud of our humility! In fact, someone has said that we can't try to be humble, for the thought in itself shows we really are not. William Law, an English cleric of the 18th century, wrote, "You can have no greater sign of confirmed pride than when you think you are humble enough."

My dad was a water-well driller who barely made enough to

cover expenses, never owned but one suit in his life, drove an old 1954 GMC pickup until it fell apart, and built much of our home from second-hand lumber. He had little use for men who worked in offices and didn't have grease under their fingernails and calluses on their hands. He was a man of complete integrity, and I adored him.

A bratty kid, I could get away with telling him almost anything. One day I said, "Dad, you're so proud of being humble!" He pretended to frown, but I saw him nodding to himself as he walked away. He had to think about what I said. My sassiness had hit home.

Growing up in an environment so critical of others left its mark on my basic nature, and God continually reveals new evidences of pride that I need to release. Pride is like the many-headed serpent Hydra that Hercules had to slay. For every proud attitude I conquer, two more seem to appear.

Too often, I have found myself critical of those who lack my family's strong work ethic, maligning them in my thoughts as "lazy." When God brought this to my attention, I prayed, "Change my heart, O Lord!"

He answered, *This is a thick layer of self-deceit born of a poor but hardworking family. There are probably no prouder people than these nor more prone to judge others. Those who rise above poor beginnings fall prey to this great sin of judgment and pride. Pride divides!"*

Legalism

As Neil Anderson teaches in his book *Breaking the Bondage of Legalism,*[1] trying to win favor with God by our performance and adhering to non-biblical rules and regulations is a great danger. Jesus came to give us freedom and grace, setting us free from the heavy burdens of man-made "dos" and "don'ts," and our many misguided attempts to find holiness. "Take My yoke upon you and learn from Me," He said, "for I am gentle and humble in heart, and you will find rest for your souls. For

My yoke is easy and my burden is light" (Matthew 11:29-30).

A great deal of false pride comes of trying to reach our own or others' standards. Much of Saint Paul's writings are directed against the legalism that crept into the early Church.

If we meet our self-imposed rules, we become proud, and our self-righteousness separates us from others. If we cannot, we feel inferior and, again, are separated from others. True freedom in Christ brings fellowship, compassion, and acceptance of ourselves and others.

Prejudice

Jane Austen, the 19th century novelist, chose a great title for one of her stories—*Pride and Prejudice*. There is much truth in the yoking of the two terms. Prejudice—the sin of pre-judging others—is the ugly offspring of pride.

In the third chapter of Colossians, Saint Paul commands us to rid ourselves of anger, rage, malice, slander, filthy language, lying, and prejudice. I patted myself on the back for having overcome most of this list until I came to the last item—prejudice. God strongly convicted me, saying, *"The other sins are sins of youth and early maturity. Prejudice is one that gains a stronger foothold the older you grow."*

I don't want to become a prejudiced, opinionated old person. I want to see Christ as all and in all, looking past people's outward appearance or personality and listening to their hearts. Make me more like You, Lord!

I love Dottie Rambo's song "He Looked Beyond My Fault," [2] which beautifully describes God's grace to this undeserving sinner. One day, I penciled a second verse to express the cry of my heart:

> May I reach out to others with this grace divine
> That sees the hurting heart behind the deed;
> That will ignore the surly look and angry words,
> Like Christ, see through the fault to touch the need.

Contempt

As we continue listening to His voice, He will reveal many unrecognized areas of pride that we must release. The Bible tells us pride and arrogance lead to captivity (Jeremiah 13:17). A recent journal entry of God's voice reads, *"Joanne, pride is the greatest sin. It certainly will destroy you. You weep over your captivity, and yet fail to repent of all your pride. I am bringing you into repentance, to be willing to let go of every pride—those secret prides that you cherish."*

Then the Lord pointed out the deep contempt I held for a young man convicted of multiple murders. He showed me that the youth was himself a victim, enslaved in body, mind, emotions, and spirit to the evil desires of an older man. God said that I was not given this discernment to "spit upon" the boy, but rather to repent of my arrogance and to intercede for him. *"The opposite of antipathy is compassion,"* He said.

I had no idea the meaning of "antipathy" when God gave me this word, and I had to look it up in my thesaurus. These are the meanings I found: dislike, aversion, distaste, disgust, repulsion, loathing, repugnance, abhorrence, antagonism, animosity, ill will, enmity, rancor, hostility, unfriendliness. None of these were adjectives I wanted describing me.

I have never prayed for an accused murderer before, yet, with God's help, I prayed with complete sincerity and earnestness— not for the young man's freedom or escape from punishment, but for his redemption.

Then He said, *"Joanne, do you see how pervasive your pride is, equally as enslaving as this young man's bondage has been? Are you willing to be different from those all around you, to have unpopular opinions, to be misunderstood and allow misunderstanding of you—to be free of the roots of pride that wrap their tentacles around your mind, your emotions, your body, and your soul?"*

I have never felt the presence of God more strongly, nor have

I ever been more assured of His love. His correction is sweeter than all the praise people could heap upon me.

Compassion

Compassion is the antithesis of pride. It is the hallmark of Christ and mankind's greatest need. Yet how hard it is to sustain.

Every year, our world suffers disasters of biblical proportions, with the death toll almost too much for our minds to comprehend. Almost every month, we hear of hundreds of thousands killed and millions left homeless by tsunamis, hurricanes, and earthquakes. Record-breaking rainfall brings misery to one part of our world, while droughts trigger wildfires in others. All the while, armed conflicts oppress and terrorize innocent people.

When so much happens to so many, our hearts threaten to become callused. At last, the terrible earthquake in the mountains of Pakistan, where over 70,000 died, awakened me to the dullness of my heart, and I prayed, "Lord Jesus, forgive me. I have not cared. I have not dipped into my own pocket to help others who are in misery, shivering in the cold, hungry as I have never been. Change my heart, Lord. Make me willing to change! What would You have me do? What can I do?"

I felt that He answered, *"Caring is where it begins. You cannot be of any use to My kingdom unless you give Me your heart."*

Make these words of Saint Francis of Assisi my prayer, O Lord:

Lord, make me an instrument of thy peace.
Where there is hatred, let me sow love;
Where there is injury, pardon;
Where there is doubt, faith;
Where there is despair, hope;
Where there is darkness, light;

Where there is sadness, joy.
O divine Master,
Grant that I may not so much seek
To be consoled as to console,
To be understood as to understand,
To be loved, as to love;
For it is in giving that we receive;
It is in pardoning that we are pardoned;
It is in dying to self that we are born to eternal life.

Feet of clay

Probably the greatest pride-breakers and the most painful are those times when we find ourselves doing things we have repented of and turned away from long ago.

I know God leads me, and I know He protects me from most of my own foolishness. Several years ago, however, He let my feet slip, and my actions brought disgrace to my family and to His name. Although I sought and received His forgiveness, I still struggled with forgiving myself, and the "whys" kept playing through my mind. "Why, Lord, why did You let me do that? Why didn't You stop me?"

At last, with great gentleness, He began to show me that I had become self-righteous in my Christian walk. It was necessary to show me that my feet were as clay-filled as the next person's. I agree with Saint Paul: "Nothing good lives in me" (Romans 7:18). In myself, I am nothing.

As a result, I am less tempted to judge others. He gave me these words: *"I want no arrogance in you regarding your comfortable life, family, or abilities. Scorn no one. Remember, there but for My grace, go you."*

Listening prayer

Do you feel a division between yourself and others? Are you

guilty of judging those who are less "righteous" than you? Can you accept one who has fallen into immorality, knowing that only God has the full story?

Use your prayer journal to ask Him to reveal and cleanse from hateful pride.

CHAPTER 12

Overcoming Guilt

GODLY SORROW BRINGS REPENTANCE
THAT LEADS TO SALVATION AND LEAVES NO REGRET,
BUT WORLDLY SORROW BRINGS DEATH.

~ 2 CORINTHIANS 7:10

There's a story told of a sweet old lady on her deathbed, surrounded by eight adoring children who had gathered to be with her in her last hours. When she fell into a deep coma, the doctor advised them that the end was very near.

They were startled when she opened her eyes and gasped, "Is it really true that God forgives sin?"

"Of course, He does, Mama," her son assured her, wiping her forehead.

A second time she begged them, "Are you sure? Do you really believe God forgives all sin?"

The children again tried to reassure her, and she fell back into a troubled sleep.

Again, she woke and looked around with wide, desperate eyes, demanding, "God does forgive our sin when we ask Him to, doesn't He?"

After they finally calmed her, the children looked at one another in astonishment. What could be causing their wonderful mother such anxiety? One of the daughters leaned over the old woman and shouted in her ear, "What sin, Mama? What are you talking about?"

The old lady glared and snapped, "None of your business!" Without another word, she closed her eyes and lapsed back into her coma.

Most of us can relate to this story. We've done a few things we'd rather our kids never knew about. However, they wouldn't be too surprised. They've probably figured out we're not perfect.

The great news is: yes, God does forgive our sins! He takes them as far from us as the east is from the west, and remembers them no more (Psalm 103:12). This is the great mystery that is incomprehensible to the human mind, that if we confess our sins, He is faithful and just and will forgive our sins, and—even more incredible—will purify us from all unrighteousness! (1 John 1:9). It's as simple as that!

Real guilt vs. False guilt

The feeling of guilt when we've broken God's laws is very painful. It will rob us of sleep and destroy our lives. When David committed adultery with Bathsheba and arranged for the murder of her husband, he was miserable. "When I kept silent, my bones wasted away through my groaning all day long. For day and night, Your hand was heavy upon me; my strength was sapped as in the heat of summer" (Psalm 32:3-4).

Even though David was a powerful king, God did not let him get away with his sin. When the prophet Nathan confronted him, David confessed, "I have sinned against the Lord." He could not undo what he had done, but it was necessary for him to confess and be forgiven. Then he could sing, "Blessed is the one whose transgressions are forgiven, whose sins are covered. Blessed is the one whose sin the Lord does not count against him and in whose spirit is no deceit" (Psalm 32:1-2). True guilt is designed to drive us back into a right relationship with God. He requires us to take responsibility for our actions, confess the wrong, make restitution if possible, and walk through the consequences a changed person.

Chuck Colson, one of the dirtiest politicians of the Nixon Administration, shocked the nation with his conversion to Christianity. He became one of Christianity's recent heroes, because he faced his guilt, took it to God, and walked out of prison a far better man. The organization he founded upon his release, Prison Fellowship Ministries, is now the world's largest outreach to prisoners and their families.

False guilt is that which, rather than bringing us to our knees, drives us further away from God. False guilt tells a man, because he has failed to live up to a church's legalistic standards, he has failed at being a Christian and may as well give up. It is a trap from which there is no promise of freedom in Christ.

Another trap is that of trying too hard for acceptance from others and from God. This person cannot rest, for in relaxing they let down their guard. They must continually work to gain acceptance. "In vain you rise early and stay up late, toiling for food to eat—for He grants sleep to those He loves" (Psalm 127:2).

Victims of abuse are particularly prone to taking upon themselves the blame for another's actions. The spouse of an abusive alcoholic is apt to say, "Well, I provoked him. If I had acted differently, he wouldn't have gone to the bar and gotten drunk. I knew better than to criticize him for spending all our money. So it's my fault that he beat me up."

A girl who has been sexually abused may blame herself for not stopping the attack or for wearing revealing clothing.

A good support group will help work through the illogic of these feelings, until you can hear the words from your Heavenly Father. *"Beloved, you are not to blame!"*

Manipulative guilt

Q. How many Jewish mothers does it take to change a light bulb?

A. None. "Don't mind me. I'll just sit here in the dark." [1]

We manipulate our children to get them to eat their spinach. We manipulate ourselves to stay on our diets. We women manipulate our husbands by silence or, even worse, by weeping. Manipulation is a way of trying to gain control over others, and it's never appropriate.

At the risk of rewriting the Bible, I can imagine Salome, the mother of the Apostles James and John, using a little "Jewish-mother" manipulation to coerce them to go with her and ask Jesus for special honors. They probably resisted, for Jesus had already told them they would be rewarded. But she would not be satisfied.

I imagine her sighing and looking toward heaven. One argument never failed. She held up her hands in mock resignation, her expression one of patient endurance.

"Enough! I will say no more. If you do not wish to give your mother this pleasure, if you do not wish to honor the memory of your father, that is your choice." Then she pretended not to see the look that passed between her sons, the one that said, "We might as well do as she says. We'll have no peace until we do."

Absence of guilt

"Let your conscience be your guide," an old saying goes. The problem is, as Billy Graham points out, most of us use our consciences as wheelbarrows, pushing them ahead of us in the direction we want them to go. [2] The moral compass that God built into us can become seared until the only regret we feel is when we get caught. Human compassion and kindness dwindles, and "both their minds and consciences are corrupted. They claim to know God, but by their actions they deny him" (Titus 1:15-16).

I fear that our country is becoming filled with people who have no remorse for the consequences of their behavior. They may be highly intelligent, yet be manipulative or deceitful in order to achieve their selfish desires. Rules and laws are for other people, not for them. When this is seen even in our leaders and we find ourselves accepting their behavior, we are in deep trouble.

Where did conscience come from? Is it only the remembered voices of Mommy and Daddy, still imposing their rules upon us? No, it's much deeper than that. Realization of wrongdoing came into the world with Adam and Eve's first bite of the forbidden fruit. They knew they had disobeyed God. But who told them they were naked?

In fact, teaching cannot totally obliterate the messages that God has printed on our consciences. No matter how sexually "liberated" our culture becomes, a girl knows when she allows herself to be seduced, it is wrong. She may marry the man, but she will never have the respect for him that she would have had he waited until their wedding night. [3]

Even though conscience is something God builds into us, we can ignore it until, like the Cretans in Paul's letter to Titus, it doesn't work anymore. However, by looking into the Word of God, we can retrain our thinking. "Do not conform any longer to the pattern of this world, but be transformed by the renewing of your mind. Then you will be able to test and approve what God's will is—His good, pleasing and perfect will" (Romans 12:2).

If you recognize that your heart and mind have been hardened by repeatedly ignoring your conscience, soak in the Word. Use your listening prayer journal to ask for God to be your guide. He promises, "Whether you turn to the right or to the left, your ears will hear a voice behind you, saying, 'This is the way; walk in it'" (Isaiah 30:21).

Let that always be our prayer.

Punishment of self or others

Is guilt bad? Our modern culture would have us believe so. People spend thousands of hours in therapy and millions of dollars trying to rid themselves of tormenting consciences. "Don't lay a guilt trip on me," has become today's banner. Yet we read with disgust of a psychopath who shows no remorse

for his crimes. We want others to be sorry for their sins, but don't blame us for ours. No wonder we're sick!

Unless guilt over past sins is dealt with, we will continue trying to either punish ourselves or others. The moral code we all inherited from Adam and Eve tells us that if someone does wrong, he must pay. We spend a great deal of useless energy trying to settle these old debts. This is why we punish ourselves with depression, overwork, repeated accidents, self-induced sickness, or failures in our work or relationships.

If we're not of a nature to kick ourselves, we may punish those around us. Men who abuse their wives and children are probably acting out of hidden feelings of guilt. The people who rudely push ahead of you in line or cut you off on the freeway may be trying to cover anger at themselves.

Old regrets eat at us and lead us into addictions to escape the pain of our past. **We cannot endure our guilty hearts.**

Even those who have turned their lives around and live impeccable lives have trouble believing that youthful sin can be forgiven. Nothing but the blood of Jesus and His remarkable grace will relieve us of this terrible burden. The words of a centuries-old hymn, "Rock of Ages," describe perfectly our dilemma:

"Could my tears forever flow,
All for sin could not atone;
Thou must save, and Thou alone." [4]

Repentance

Repentance is a necessary step to salvation. It is much more than regret. "I'm sorry, God, that I sinned" won't do. Anyone can mouth those words, hoping to escape eternal damnation, and still be unsaved. Neither can we atone for our sin by layers of good works. On the great day of judgment, unless we have a personal relationship with Christ, He will say, "I never knew you. Away from me, you evildoers!" (Matthew 7:23).

True repentance is deep godly sorrow as we look at our lives, recognizing the damage we have done to ourselves and to others, and viewing our unrighteousness in the holy light of Jesus. Repentance is an outgrowth of the Holy Spirit's conviction. He, and He alone, can bring us to this valley of sorrow for our sins.

At the age of sixteen, a rebellious teenager, I was invited to a youth revival by a friend. When the evangelist preached, "Don't Set Sail on the Sea of Sin," my heart was convicted, and I raised my hand for prayer. Summoned to kneel at the old wooden altar, I gave way to weeping as God held a mirror up before me and showed me the hurt I was causing my parents and the mess I was making of my life. Almost a box of tissues later, I rose to my feet and made my way home.

I had no idea what had happened to me, but within two weeks, people were asking, "Is that the same girl?" My rebellious ways and lying slipped away. I began going to church night after night, making new friends and weaving a new life. The repentance I experienced that evening resulted in a complete turning away from sin to follow Christ.

Sometimes repentance is spiritual surgery, for the things we have carried many years have deep roots. As a mature adult, I still harbored the sin of a quick, quarrelsome tongue. No one could win an argument with me. One night, I woke to find my husband tossing and turning. "What's wrong, Tommy?" I asked.

He gave a deep sigh. "I only wish you hadn't argued with Mrs. Gilmore today."

Oh, my! I saw myself in God's mirror again, and it was not a pretty sight. I chewed on the problem for several days before finally spending an afternoon on my knees. In tears, I begged God to remove not only the sin, but also the deep roots of ugly pride that surrounded it.

Thank God, He answered my prayer. Quarreling is no longer a defense I feel the need to use. Now I can discuss an issue or situation without the determination to come out a winner. I like myself better and know I'm much more pleasant to be around.

Grace

Grace is the great message of the Gospel. Not one of us deserves God's favor, for if our lives, our motives, our words, and our inmost thoughts were exposed, who could stand? Yet, even as Moses raised the bronze serpent in the wilderness to save those bitten by venomous snakes, God raised up Jesus and asks that we reach out to Him. We've been bitten by sin, and it's deadly. No amount of good works can save us. No self-flagellation will free us.

God built a bridge over the chasm between heaven and its holiness and earth and its sinfulness. This Bridge is Jesus, and we are all invited to cross over, regardless of our sinful condition. We do not have to work for our salvation. It is a free gift of God! This is the truth that blew Martin Luther away and ushered in the Protestant Reformation. "For it is by grace you have been saved, through faith—and this not from yourselves, it is the gift of God—not by works, so that no one can boast" (Ephesians 2:8-9).

My father had trouble accepting this truth. Acutely aware of his many faults, he could not imagine God would forgive him so easily. I smile when I think how surprised he must have been when he got to heaven and realized that his prayer of confession, accepting Jesus as Lord, washed away all the guilt he carried for so many years.

Will you accept His grace? Will you let Him wash you clean of all guilt, either real or imagined?

CHAPTER 13

Overcoming Shame

IN YOU, LORD MY GOD, I PUT MY TRUST.
I TRUST IN YOU;
DO NOT LET ME BE PUT TO SHAME,
NOR LET MY ENEMIES TRIUMPH OVER ME.
~ PSALM 25:1-2

We tend to think of shame as with guilt, but in reality, the two terms are much different. Shame is like Velcro, clinging to our spirits long after we have received God's forgiveness.

Guilt focuses on specific sinful deeds. We know we did something wrong, and we feel we should be punished. We can make restitution to those we have hurt, as the tax collector Zacchaeus did, repaying the money he had extorted from his fellow countrymen. We may have to pay our debt to society by spending time in prison, but when those days/months/years are finished, we can walk away, knowing the guilt is behind us. Finally, we can take our wrongdoing to the cross of Jesus, repent with a sincere heart, and be assured that He will forgive us and cleanse us from our unrighteousness (1 John 1:9).

Shame goes deeper. It tells us, "You're a bad person." It's a nebulous feeling that often cannot be pinpointed to any one particular incident.

A great deal of shame is carried from childhood, when we may have been called "bad" for some childish mistake. Young minds and hearts are much more susceptible to words spoken in irritation or anger than adults realize. Children are quick to accept the worst possible connotation of words.

Unthinking about the pain she caused, my mother used to call me "a little hellion" when I irritated her. Many years and hurt feelings later, I realized the word meant "a mischievous child" rather than a child of hell.

Children of divorce often carry unwarranted shame because their parents did not stay married. One of my good friends relates the shame she felt because her mother and father did not love each other. As a small child unable to understand where the blame lay, she took it upon herself. "It's my fault. If I had been prettier or more loveable, my mother wouldn't have left us."

Victims of rape or molestation carry the deepest shame of all. The perpetrator, unable to face his own guilt, may transfer the blame. "It's your fault. If you wouldn't dress like a tramp, etc." If the child tells, the mother may be unable to process the horror of the deed. "Not my husband! He's a good man!" "Not my son Johnny! He wouldn't do something like that!" So she does nothing, perhaps accusing the child of lying. But under the surface, the anxiety brews and the mistrust grows. The family is caught in a terrible secret that traps the child in its ever-deepening web.

Shame is the most painful of emotions and one which we cannot hide, although, like Adam and Eve, we try. Somehow, other people can sense our hidden feelings. I believe there is something sadistic in humans that senses another's shame and attracts mistreatment. Little chickens will peck to death another baby chick when it is injured. Likewise, girls who have been molested often find themselves in abusive relationships as adults. If a poll could be taken of women who have to seek safety from domestic violence, chances are that the greater percent will have suffered sexual abuse as a child. Of women who are raped as adults, I've been told that the majority attest to having been molested as children.

Some of us try to cover up our shame, becoming over-achievers, workaholics, party animals, flashy dressers, etc. Like the proverbial clown, as soon as the artificial mask is removed, the pain returns.

Shifting the blame to others is another tactic we use to deal with shame. We develop a judgmental, self-righteous attitude to camouflage our imperfection. God never lets me get away with this. Criticizing others seems to work until I realize that four of my fingers are pointing back at myself.

Last of all, we try to excuse ourselves. "It wasn't my fault." "If I'd had a different set of parents," etc. The trouble is, we know these are lies even as we voice them.

Listening prayer can help us identify the shame we try to hide, cover up, blame others for, or excuse.

Use your journal to ask God, "What behaviors are keeping me from the abundant life Jesus promised?" (John 10:10). He may show you several defense mechanisms that are holding you in bondage.

Then ask, "Am I doing these things to hide my shame?" A picture or an old feeling may come to mind that will help identify the memory. If you find yourself weeping, your tears are an indication that you are very near the source of your pain. Let Him help you. He is the Great Physician, and this is spiritual surgery. An abscess must be exposed to the light and drained to bring healing.

Ask, "Was I to blame, Lord?"

Whatever the truth, there will be great healing in His words. Chances are, you will see yourself in the memory through new eyes, as an innocent, vulnerable child. You will feel awe as you understand that the sin was not yours. You may even feel pity for the perpetrator, knowing that he will face God's wrath. Jesus said, "It will be better for him to have a large millstone hung around his neck and to be drowned in the depths of the sea" (Matthew 18:6).

Even if God answers, "Yes, Beloved, you were at fault, in that you did such-and-such," He will wash away the shame and forgive your guilt. At last, the truth will set you free (John 8:32).

You may want to ask Jesus to walk with you back through the memory and let His presence protect you and reassure you.

The hard question remains: "Jesus, why did You let this happen?" He does not interfere with human choice and free will, even for those who hurt little children. But we can be assured, not only in knowing they will be punished in God's time, but also that He can use even our wounds for good.

The scars of our shame

I worked at Shriners Burn Institute in Galveston for several years as a medical records librarian and learned a great deal about the devastation that burns cause. The wonderful staff of dedicated doctors, nurses, and therapists committed themselves not only to keeping the children alive, but also to prevent the resulting scars from becoming crippling deformities. The best treatment, they found, was to keep pressure on the scar tissue and to use physical therapy to force the child to exercise the affected area.

I see in this a wonderful analogy for our spiritual and emotional wounds. Scar tissue deforms because it's stronger than our natural tissue. If we try to hide those things that have caused us shame, we become crippled. As we let Jesus show us how to expose these old scars, they will become the strongest part of our character and our greatest testimony.

I think of Beth Moore and Joyce Meyers, both of whom have shared the sexual abuse they suffered as children. Their willingness to expose those emotional scars has ministered to thousands of other women.

It's uncomfortable, but the only solution is to quit hiding our shame, bring it to Jesus, and allow Him to use us in His service. Like Thomas, we can touch the nail prints in His hands and find them beautiful. The late Dr. Paul Brand marveled that Jesus's glorified body retained His scars. "He carried the marks of suffering so He could continue to understand the needs of those suffering. He wanted to be forever one with us." [1]

God doesn't take our dark memories away, but He heals the pain and asks us to use our scarred lives to bless others, to comfort them "with the comfort we ourselves have received from God" (2 Corinthians 1:4).

We need not continue hanging our heads or pretending to have lived perfect lives. Jesus took all of our shame upon Himself when He was despised and rejected (Isaiah 53:3), spit upon, mocked, beaten, stripped naked, and nailed to a cross to die a criminal's death.

Because He is King of kings and risen Lord of lords, He can take our shame and cover it with one of the mightiest word in all creation—GRACE. By His grace, we can shed our garments of shame and be given new life in Him. Satan's mocking voice will be stilled forever. Instead of our shame, we will receive a double portion of God's favor. Instead of disgrace, we will rejoice with an everlasting joy (Isaiah 61:7).

Will you leave your shame at His cross and receive the beautiful robe of His grace right now?

CHAPTER 14

Overcoming Depression

A HEALTHY SPIRIT CONQUERS ADVERSITY,
BUT WHAT CAN YOU DO WHEN THE SPIRIT IS CRUSHED?
~ PROVERBS 18:14, MSG

Depression has been described as anger turned inward or grief that cannot be consoled. While almost everyone experiences some symptoms occasionally, there are others for whom keeping out of "the pits" of hopelessness and despair is a lifelong struggle. Statistics show that depression is the leading cause of disability in the United States.[1] It affects about sixteen percent of all people, both Christian and non-Christian, during their lives. It is usually marked by feelings of sadness or hopelessness, low energy, and an inability to feel pleasure for an extended period of time. However, it may also show up as aggression, substance abuse, and/or eating disorders.

Depression affects loved ones

Serious depression can disrupt not only the life of the sufferer, but also the lives of those he or she loves. If you have never experienced the emotional impact and severity of this disorder, it may be hard for you to understand when a family member or friend cannot seem to bounce back. What they are feeling is much worse than just "having the blues" or "being down." Lack of understanding may make the depressed individual feel extreme guilt, adding an additional burden to an already too-heavy load.

Anti-depression medications

There are many medications available which ease the depth or duration of negative feelings. So long as anti-depressants are prescribed by an excellent doctor who carefully monitors them, I do not believe there should be any guilt attached to their use. They should never be discontinued without medical consultation. Remember, depression is not a character flaw or a sign of personal weakness.

Is depression mentioned in the Bible?

Many of our great Bible heroes have suffered bouts of depression. King David certainly did after he committed adultery. Psalm 32:3 records his misery. "When I kept silent, my bones wasted away through my groaning all day long." Psalm 38 shows a heart weighed down under a load of guilt:

"My guilt has overwhelmed me like a burden too heavy to bear. My wounds fester and are loathsome because of my sinful folly. I am bowed down and brought very low; all day long I go about mourning.... My heart pounds, my strength fails me; even the light has gone from my eyes.... I confess my iniquity; I am troubled by my sin....O Lord, do not forsake me; be not far from me, O my God. Come quickly to help me, O Lord my Savior."

His humble prayer for forgiveness recorded in Psalm 51:10 is an example to every believer. "Create in me a pure heart, O God, and renew a steadfast spirit within me." If God can forgive an adulterer and murderer such as David, He will forgive you and me.

Jonah, Job, Elijah, and Jeremiah also went through periods of hopelessness and despair. In turning to God, they received comfort and direction.

Several Bible characters did not seek answers from God, and their anger turned into violent aggression toward others or themselves. Cain's anger accelerated into the murder of his brother. King Saul's melancholy spirit incited hatred toward David. Judas turned his misery inward and committed suicide.

Is there a reason for depression?

Physical pain can be our greatest ally by signaling us of an injury to a part of our body. Dr. Paul Brand, who worked with leprosy patients, tells of those who have lost entire fingers because they could not feel the bite of a rat. [2] Their bodies have lost the warning system that alerts us to bodily dangers.

Depression, like physical pain, is a symptom of something God wants us to address. His design in our discomfort is to demand a change in response to danger. Dr. Brand writes, "Emotional and spiritual pain are, like physical pain, symptoms and not diseases. Normally, a symptom will not disappear until the disease is treated." [3]

Listening prayer

Listening prayer can be a valuable tool to help find the way out of the darkness of depression. For many years, my daughter suffered recurrent episodes that took away her energy and her motivation. She found that if she asked God, "What one thing can I do?" and listened for His answer, He gave the direction she needed. If only, *"Get dressed,"* or *"Make your bed,"* obedience in these simple tasks seemed to break the overwhelming log jam that crushed her spirit.

Guilt will weigh upon our minds if it is not addressed. As it saps our joy, we feel depressed because our lives are not working. Then we feel guilty because we see our depression affecting others. Only as we bring the matter to God and ask for forgiveness and cleansing can we break this vicious cycle.

My dear friend Bette is one of the most joyful, productive people I know, on fire for Christ. Yet she spent sixteen years incapacitated by depression. A doctor who worked at her psychiatric hospital told me that she was so withdrawn, no one could communicate with her.

She gave me permission to share her story of how God healed her as she listened to Him and obeyed, step by step.

I think I was depressed most of my life, but I thought my feelings were normal. I had been abused for a long time very early in my life, but I accepted this as normal. When the pain was the greatest, I would retreat into the arms of Jesus in my mind. There I was safe and comforted.

Then, as a teen, I became more depressed. My family life had deteriorated before my eyes, and I felt deep rejection. I became bitter with the world because I felt I had been cheated of a family emotionally. But I moved on, attending college and then into a career.

Later in my life, I was held up at gunpoint while working. I became unable to work, paralyzed with fear as the robber stalked me for weeks afterward. That's when I sought professional counseling and later went into a hospital in order to get medication to help me cope.

During therapy I became aware that I had been sexually abused. At one point I addressed one of the individuals involved, asking if it was true. I desperately wanted that person to say no so I could continue in my fantasy that everything was great and my life had been 'normal.' When that didn't happen and there was no concrete denial, I went wild with self-anger and hatred. I had been faithful to God's calling, working hard in our church, teaching classes and conducting retreats. I had done what God had called me to do, yet, with all this horrible information about my past, how could I continue thinking of myself as a person of good character? I felt like life was a horrible joke! I was so angry, so full of shame and self-hatred that I became suicidal.

Years later, after having been on every antidepressant on the market, I could no longer function and was tired of pretending that I could. I had reached the bottom. There were no pills to lift my mood, no doctor or therapist to give the right counsel, and no program or solution to relieve this burden that I had carried almost all my life. I had done everything prescribed to me by the professionals, but I no longer wanted to live. Life was no longer of any value.

I threw away my pills and told God that I'd had enough. I understood the consequences of sudden withdrawal from the medication but no longer cared. Life had become unbearable, and I was willing to risk death to escape the inner hell I lived in. I asked God for something—anything. I could not go on. I heard no response, but believed He was there.

That night, I went to bed as usual. Two

or three uneventful days passed. Then He started waking me up at 2:00 a.m. every day for two weeks when the house was quiet and there were no interruptions. He spoke to me of my life and of His love. He was very gentle, without a word of criticism, only instruction and encouragement. He told me that He was not displeased with me, but there were changes He wanted me to make. There would be more required of me.

Daily, He gave a new list of things to do—take a walk, drink more water, eat healthy, etc. After I accomplished those, He would give another the next night. During these little 2:00 a.m. 'chats,' He did all the talking, while I listened.

One of the key things He instructed me to do was to resume a serious, deep Bible study. Before I became so depressed, I studied the Bible a lot, and I missed that opportunity and privilege.

I have to admit, this demand seemed a bit crazy to me. While I had no problem taking God at His word or believing in His faithfulness, I had been unable to comprehend anything I read. All the medication I had been taking confused my mind. However, I believed I should follow His instruction no matter if it seemed senseless, and do it without question. Perhaps, I thought, He was just comforting me. Little did I realize that the Word heals. 'My son, attend to my words; consent and submit to my sayings. Let them not depart from your sight; keep them in the center of your heart. For they are life to those who find them, healing and health to all their flesh' (Proverbs 4:20-22, AMP).

I am convinced without any doubt that my healing from depression, guilt, shame, and everything else is connected to studying the Word. As I began to write Scripture verses and speak them out loud, I was healed. It was a process of nine months, but the healing in undeniable and has never faltered.

I'll never understand why He healed me other than His love and mercy. I know I am completely undeserving of such love. He is simply so BIG and I am so small. I have always been a very quiet person, inhibited in many ways, but the miracle of my healing completely altered my life and my thinking. I have always felt His loving hand around me, but now you will see me jump while worshipping. I promised myself that in every service, every time I come before Him, I would give Him one hundred percent, holding nothing back.

He has kept His word about requiring more of me. He does daily. But His love never fades. He is good to me, and I am totally dependent upon Him. He is truly my breath...and my love.

Bette also told me how God asked her to walk some every day, despite her physical weakness from years of inactivity. First, He asked her to walk to the front of the house, then to the neighbor's house, and then around the block. Now she walks two miles every day and is strong and healthy.

Once an accomplished musician, she would not touch a musical instrument during her hospitalization. Now she is an active member of her church's praise team, often playing her keyboard for other ministries as well.

When you feel depressed

I have never suffered myself from lengthy depressions. However, I have witnessed not only its devastating effects in my family, but also the healing that God brings. So, even though I'm not a medical expert, I can offer a few suggestions from the experience of friends and loved ones:

1. Begin reading a chapter from the Psalms daily, asking God to show you His love and His presence. Don't be afraid of your emotions. Pour them out to Him. David was a very emotional person, and the Bible says he was a man after God's own heart (1 Samuel 13:14).

2. Write in your prayer journal the insights God gives you as you read His Word. Express your thoughts and feelings in writing. Someone has wisely said, "Impression without expression equals depression." Conversely, expressing the impressions of your heart will help ward off depression.

3. Let God make your "do-list." As you obey in small things, He will enable you to do more.

4. When the weather permits, spend a little time each day enjoying His creation. Sit outside in the sun. Let Him caress you with a gentle breeze. Listen to the music of the birds. Praise Him for the beauty around you.

5. If your doctor agrees, twenty minutes of exercise several times a week will help lift your mood and make you sleep better.

6. Drink more water, particularly if you are taking medications. Isaiah 44:12 speaks of a fool who *"drinks no water and grows faint."*

7. Eat more Omega-3 fatty acids, found naturally in oily fish, flax seeds, hemp seeds, walnuts, and canola oils. These have been found to be effective as a dietary supplement. [4]

8. Seek help from other Christians. A recommended web site is *www.godlife.com*, which can put you in contact with a Christian by e-mail for free, private assistance.

CHAPTER 15

Overcoming Anger

REFRAIN FROM ANGER AND TURN FROM WRATH;
DO NOT FRET—IT LEADS ONLY TO EVIL.
~ PSALM 37:8

Of all the obstacles to hearing God's voice, anger is the most dangerous. Someone has noted that "anger" is just one letter away from "danger." Yet the Bible does not call anger in itself a sin. In Ephesians 4:26, Saint Paul advises, "In your anger, do not sin."

In the first book of the Bible, we read how Cain was filled with anger because his offering was not shown as much favor as his brother's. The Lord tried to counsel Cain, saying, "Why are you angry? Why is your face downcast? If you do what is right, will you not be accepted? But if you do not do what is right, sin is crouching at your door; it desires to have you, but you must rule over it" (Genesis 4:6-7). Instead of responding, Cain reacted, and he committed the world's first murder.

We stand in Cain's shoes when we feel the first flush of anger. If we are in the habit of going to God every morning and listening for His voice, He will correct us. Then, if we listen and **respond** to His correction, we can conquer our emotions. We can even learn something from the situation. Unfortunately, too often we **react**, like Cain, justifying ourselves and lashing out to hurt another.

Righteous anger

Many people justify their temper, saying, "Well, Jesus got angry. He made a whip of cords and drove the money changers out of the Temple, overturning tables and scattering coins and caged birds and animals."

That's true. What happened to "gentle Jesus, meek and mild?" He was angry! Yet He was also sinless. When we examine the cause of His anger, we recognize that His act was altogether pure and beautiful, for it was one of selfless courage. By His action, He sealed His own death warrant.

History[1] tells us the High Priest, Annas, and his sons owned all the concessions in the Temple, and every year they charged higher and higher prices. Pilgrims who returned from the feast days told horror stories. One man who had traveled from Egypt so that his son might participate in the Passover was charged a week's wages for two small pigeons. If a worshiper thought to purchase a sacrificial lamb outside the Temple or even bring it from home, corrupt "inspectors" would find the animal defective.

The system was wrong, and everyone knew it was wrong, but no one had any power to change it. King Herod had changed the position of High Priest into a political plum, and with it came opportunities for great power and wealth. Annas took full advantage of his appointment, making his sons treasurers and his sons-in-law assistant treasurers. Within a short time, the stalls for changing money and selling sacrificial animals were moved into the Temple area itself. The Court of the Gentiles was often called the "Bazaar of the Sons of Annas." In turn, the men they hired to run this "business" became so arrogant that to disagree with them was to invite violence. They were even known to beat complainers with sticks.

When Jesus drove these unscrupulous vendors from the Temple courts, He did what every honest man in Judea wished he could do. He turned on the vendors, calling them by their rightful name, "thieves," and had them scurrying like rats, their hands over their heads in fear. In the meantime, Annas and his sons were watching, their hatred for Him growing into a murderous plot. The Galilean could not, and would not, be allowed to live.

This is the kind of righteous anger that made Todd Beamer and his fellow travelers rush the hijackers of Flight 93 when they realized it was going to be used as a bomb. It was what caused Dietrich Bonhoffer to stand against the evil deeds of the Nazi regime, at the cost of his life. This is the courage that drove Saint Telemachus[2] to leap into the gladiatorial arena and try to push the combatants apart, shouting "This is wrong!"

It is this life-risking anger that changes the world.

Resentment

Resentment is anger that is held inside us, brewing and embittering us against the one who has wronged us or our loved ones. This is the bitterness referred to in Hebrews 12:15. "See to it that no one falls short of the grace of God and that no bitter root grows up to cause trouble and defile many."

Holding on to resentment is like grabbing a hot coal to throw at someone you're angry with. You're the one who gets burned. Even more so, the people in your life whom you dearly love are cheated. Bitterness fills up your emotional reservoir so that even trivial situations cause your anger to splash over onto those around you.

When I decided to let go of an old wall of resentment toward my brother, my children—from whom I had carefully hidden my feelings—benefited in surprising ways. They told me they sensed a new joy in me. I gained freedom to give them untarnished love. There can be no abundant life when our hearts are marred with bitterness.

When my young granddaughters lived with me for several years, I became resentful because they didn't keep my house as neat as I liked. Then one morning I made the choice to forgive them, no matter if beds were never made or clothes put away, and no matter if the living room remained a mess. As soon as I verbalized the words of forgiveness, the Holy Spirit swept over me in waves of living water, filling me with indescribable joy.

Little resentments can creep in to our unconscious minds unless the Lord reveals them. This is a great benefit of listening prayer. Very recently, He showed me that I was frustrated and a bit angry because a phone call had not been returned. In my journal, He pointed out that the other person hosted a church group in his home. *He may have been leading someone to Me. Was the phone call more important than the lost being saved?"*

Hidden anger

In addition to rage, anger may be expressed as "slander, filthy language, and lies" (Colossians 3:8). We may be too "nice" to indulge in these sins, but anger cannot be hidden. Someone has said there is no such thing as unexpressed anger. Sooner or later it will reveal itself in ulcers, hypertension, or other physical ailments. Even more often it shows itself as depression.

We may try to hide our angry feelings from others, because "a Christian shouldn't feel this way." We even deny them to ourselves, with the result being passive aggression—oversleeping, forgetfulness, being chronically late, or thinly veiled sarcasm.

It's useless to try to hide anything from God. He knows us better than we know ourselves. "Before a word is on my tongue you know it completely, O Lord" (Psalm 139:4). So talk with Him about your anger. He will help you pinpoint the source, so that you don't take out your feelings on innocent people. Then, by the power of the Holy Spirit, He will give you the grace to respond in a Christ-like way.

Jesus gave us very specific instructions on handling offenses. "If your brother or sister sins, go and point out their fault, just between the two of you. If they listen to you, you have won them over. But if they will not listen, take one or two others along, so that 'every matter may be established by the testimony of two or three witnesses.' If they still refuse to listen, tell it to the church; and if they refuse to listen even to the church, treat them as you would a pagan or a tax collector" (Matthew 18:15-17).

Listening prayer can be a wonderful tool to help apply this Scripture. If your friend or relative has said or done something to offend you, and your purpose is peaceful resolution and reconciliation, go to him. "I'm upset about this problem. Can we talk about it?" Perhaps both of you are harboring angry feelings, in which case it might be good to express them on paper before addressing each other. Seek the Holy Spirit's wisdom as you do. Listen to the other person, and you will gain a new understanding and appreciation of His heart.

An example of this happened one morning at Hidden Manna. As you can imagine, three women working in one kitchen can present problems. One busy retreat, in an effort to be helpful, I offended one of the other staff members by doing things she considered her domain. She got huffy, and I got hurt. The atmosphere became thick with tension until we found a time to practice listening prayer.

Going to separate rooms, we each poured out our feelings on paper. I'm quite verbal, especially when angry, and my complaints filled four pages. Then, as we came together and bowed to invite God's presence, I felt the familiar voice whispering to me, *"Listen to her heart."*

Reluctantly obedient, I declined the opportunity to speak first and yielded the floor. As she talked, I began to see her possessiveness about her work as an invaluable asset to our ministry. She was an employee to be prized! My view of her changed from that moment, as did her attitude toward me. I crumpled the four pages I had written and tossed them in the blazing fireplace unread. Peace was restored.

Rage

An explosive, violent temper is by far the most destructive fault that we harbor. Though often hidden from the world, our families bear the brunt of this sin. The man who wears a broad smile and offers a quick handshake may be an angry ogre to his own family. The woman who is quickest to bring a casserole to the needy may have no time or patience with her own children. "Behind closed doors" our real dispositions emerge.

The Bible is replete with admonishments against rage. "Better a patient man than a warrior, better to have self-control than to conquer a city" (Proverbs 16:32, NLT). "An angry man stirs up conflict, and a hot-tempered one commits many sins" (Proverbs 29:22). Over and over we are told that we must control the urge to let our anger fly.

My husband and I once kept a foster child who thought he could not control his temper. He would unleash it at the other children over the slightest infraction. My husband and I decided that, if the child learned nothing else, he must learn self-control. Though never advocates of physical punishment, we felt we had to administer a little pain to keep him from hurting others and eventually himself. So we made a contract with him: Every time he flew into a rage, lashing out at the other children, there would be the certainty of a spanking—administered without vindictiveness and followed by loving hugs. We only had to carry out our promise twice before the tantrums stopped.

I think God does something similar to us because He loves us. We get violent headaches or stomachaches after an outburst. A shepherd will sometimes snap the foreleg of a disobedient lamb so it cannot run away. Then he carries it over his shoulders until it is healed and has learned to stay close. How many of our physical ailments or crisis situations are the disciplining of a loving Shepherd?

What is the answer? Do we have to be slaves to a bad temper? Perhaps the key lies within the following verses: "You were taught, with regard to your former way of life, to put off your old self, which is being corrupted by its deceitful desires, to be made new in the attitude of your minds, and to put on the new self, created to be like God in true righteousness and holiness"

(Ephesians 4:22-24).

Did you catch the phrase "corrupted by its deceitful desires"? What desires are deceiving you? A desire for power over others can deceive. Many people use anger as a way of intimidating and manipulating. Whatever is the root of our anger, God will show us if we ask. Then, as we submit to His spiritual surgery, He will change us—from the inside out.

CHAPTER 16

Conquering Fears

THERE IS NO ROOM IN LOVE FOR FEAR.
WELL-FORMED LOVE BANISHES FEAR.
SINCE FEAR IS CRIPPLING, A FEARFUL LIFE—FEAR OF DEATH,
FEAR OF JUDGMENT—
IS ONE NOT YET FULLY FORMED IN LOVE.

~ 1 JOHN 4:18, MSG

The fears that most children have were never mine. In fact, it was a total lack of fear that took my ever-wandering feet to a carnival alone at the age of five. I can still feel that spanking! Most of my childhood trouble resulted from this fearlessness. Angels wisely held back, but Joanne jumped right in.

So it was rather a shock one morning to read God's message, *"My child, there is still much fear that cripples you."*

"Father, please show me my sinful fears," I prayed.

I had been studying from the book of John about the last hours of the life of Christ. Over the next few days, as I continued these same readings, my Heavenly Father revealed a few things to me.

Fear of asking and being rejected. "Ask and you will receive" (John 16:24). *"Beloved, do you not see that not to ask* rejects Me? Ask Me whatever is in your heart, and let Me sort out that which is good and that which would harm."

Fear of confrontation. "In this world you will have trouble" (John 16:33). *"Confrontation will come. The more you love Me, the less others will accept you. Do not seek confrontation, but neither shrink from it when it comes. Stand firm on the ultimate truth—Jesus Christ, Son of God, crucified for the sins of the world, risen, and now seated at the right hand of God. This truth you can live and die for. All other arguments are nonsense."*

Fear of the future. "The time has come" (John 17:1). *"Beloved, it is not yours to know the future, neither its agony nor its glory. Just take My hand and trust Me one step, one day at a time. Pour yourself out daily for Me, a little here, a little there. I am the Artist directing the whole picture. I give the direction, and I supply the resources."*

Fear of hidden doubts. "They believed that You sent Me" (John 17:6-8). *"Beloved, I am so glad you are confessing this fear. Your faith is being sifted, and it is painful. You believe the Bible as true, the witness of the disciples, and Jesus' resurrection. Yet you lack one thing: you have not yet let these beliefs color your world and turn it upside down. These trials, once they permeate your heart as well as your mind, will bring victory over every fear and every sin."*

Fear of missing the full joy. Jesus's prayer that we might share His joy (John 17:13). *"You need to do no more. Receive! Joy comes in the knowledge of My unconditional love for you. You do not have to be perfect for Me to love you. You do not have to love yourself for Me to love you. You do not have to be loved by others for Me to love you. I love you when you win, and I love you when you fail. **My love for you encompasses infinity.**"*

Fear of Satan's traps. "Protect them from the evil one" (John 17:15). *"What are the names of Satan's land mines in your life?"* That was easy! Pain, gluttony, resentment, anxiety, and anger. I was in grave danger, for I had fallen into all of those in just a few hours. He continued, *"You may feel battered* *and bashed, but remember, I can use all things for your good. Crawl out of the 'anger' hole. That is the most deadly trap. Flee it!"*

Fear of breaking promises. Judas's treachery (John 18:2-3). *"Beloved, remember that I love you immeasurably when I tell you there is some of Judas in you. He had made promises he could not keep without more money, and in desperation to protect that part of his reputation, became the world's epitome of depravity. Where is your treasure? Where are your commitments? What promises have you made that you are willing to break for My sake?"*

Fear of failing to recognize God. The soldiers fell back (John 18:6). *"Never let your do-list, your routine, or your promises blind you to the reality of My presence. The soldiers arresting Me were just 'doing their job.' They fell back because the veil hiding My glory was briefly taken away. But their job was most important to them, and they quickly returned to that role. Never let a job or your reputation as a worker be more important than Me."*

Fear of intrusion. Peter's sword (John 18:10-11). *"Beloved, you are clinging to your time as if it belonged to you, jealously guarding it against intrusion. You do not know what lies ahead for you. You do not know the cup the Father will have you drink. Look at My words to Peter, 'Put your sword away!' Lay aside your foolish defenses and your limited judgments of situations."*

Fear of glibness. Caiaphas's prediction that it would be good if one man died for the people (John 18:14). *"I want you to be very careful of the words you speak. Never let your cleverness interfere with your sincerity. Do not speak, answer, or enter into conversation in order to be considered intelligent. However, your 'two cents' can be worth a million if led by My Spirit."*

Fear of argument. Peter's first denial (John 18:15-18). *"Like Peter, often you also guard yourself or further your desires by expedient lies, half-truths, or evasiveness. You are afraid of the angry response you might get and afraid of* *getting embroiled in an argument. Search your spirit, and you can reply with My Spirit's wisdom."*

Fear of rank or class. An official striking Jesus in the face (John 18:22). *"Beloved child, put yourself in the place of the official. To him, there were ranks and classes of people. The trappings of authority were all wrapped up in long, ornate robes, haughtiness of bearing, position, and money. The Son of Man came a simple carpenter, simply dressed, and making no claims to worldly position. Strive to see each person as an individual, regardless of their age, their position, their outward appearance, or their manner of speaking. Never be guilty of snubbing another."*

Fear of challenge. Peter's denials (John 18:25-26). *"With every lie, Peter was left more vulnerable to challenge. Are you ready to be challenged? Remember that Peter's disloyalty came when he was warming himself by the fires of the world. Enjoy your non-Christian friends, but do not warm yourself by the fires of their secular perspectives."*

Fear of blame. The Jewish leaders trying to shift the blame for Jesus's death onto the Romans (John 18:28-32). *"Beloved, examine your heart. How many times have you had the impulse to shift blame to others? The seeds of the Tree of the Knowledge of Good and Evil are rooted in your heart. You don't want to be wrong, and you don't want to be blamed. Quit looking at problems and accidents to see where the fault lies. Look to the relationship. Love and forgive others just as you want to be loved and forgiven, and let Me control all."*

Fear of shading the truth. "Everyone on the side of truth listens to Me" (John 18:37). *"Beloved, My words are truth and the essence of truth. In a world of commercialism, of politics, or wars, of opposing philosophies, there will seem to be many shades of gray. Mistakes will be made by even the most earnest truth-seekers. Yet there are absolute truths that guide; e.g., sanctity of life. Learn to recognize counterfeit truth and its many layers. Go for the gold!"*

Fear of making wrong decisions. Jesus sentenced (John 19:1-6). *"Beloved, you are in Pilate's shoes every day. Every* decision that you make affects somebody else. Today, every cell in your body wants you to 'wash your hands' and retreat into your own comfort. Do not be a coward. Do what is right."

Fear of discomfort. The crucifixion (John 19:18-27). "Not only did I think of My mother while the nails tore at My flesh, the thorns pierced my forehead, and the wounds on My back tore open against the rough wood of the cross every time I pushed Myself up for air, I thought also of you. I loved you even then, and my heart was filled with compassion for you as I saw you being sifted again and again. When I prayed, 'Father, forgive them, for they know not what they do,' I was also thinking of you, that you might be forgiven for the selfishness and lack of faith that placed Me there. I was a sacrifice in your place. I suffered and died for you, Beloved."

Fear of delay. The burial of Jesus (John 19:38-42). "You want to condemn Nicodemus and Joseph of Arimathea for their cowardice in not following Me openly. Can you see them as part of the Father's perfect plan, that My body might be buried in a rich man's tomb? Because they were still prominent members of the Sanhedrin, they were able to go ask Pilate for My body. Their hearts were burning within them, for their eyes were opened. They risked their positions, their wealth, and their reputations to do this beautiful thing for Me that God laid upon their hearts. There is a time to wait and a time to act, according to My leading. Let me guide you. Do not rush into decisions until I show you. You will know when it is from Me and not your own ego."

Fear of not comprehending. The empty tomb (John 20:1-9). "The disciples had not yet recognized that God himself, the Author and Inventor of natural law, had chosen to set that law aside in order to show His great love for every one of the human race—every person into whom He has breathed life. This requires a great paradigm shift, a rebirth that transforms and changes all your expectations. What does this mean to you, Beloved?"

Joyfully, I answered, "In Your kingdom, nothing is impossible! Your natural laws need not run their course! Prayer truly changes things! Your love never fails! It means that I cannot begin to imagine what You will do this very day! This is the faith that makes all the difference!"

Fear of my own insignificance. Jesus's pre-glorification appearance to comfort Mary (John 20:10-18). *"Mary was just one woman, even as you are only one woman. Her life, too, did not qualify her for any honor. It was only her all-consuming love and devotion to Me that made her particularly precious to Me. My heart was touched by her grief. Only her heart-devotion was significant. Do you understand this, Beloved?"* Falling on my knees and weeping, I prayed, "Lord Jesus, let me love You more!"

Fear of unbelief. Thomas finally believes (John 20-24-29). *"Everyone who calls upon the name of the Lord will be saved. You have confessed Me before men as Lord. Do you believe in your heart, as well as your mind, that God raised Me from the dead?"*

I cried out, "Lord, I believe! Help my unbelief! Please fill my heart with the joy of this wonderful knowledge! Be Lord of my heart, and make a real difference in my life and in my character, I pray, Lord Jesus! Break every stronghold, and teach me how to lead others to You!"

CHAPTER 17

Overcoming Timidity

JESUS SAID, "GO OUT INTO THE HIGHWAYS AND HEDGES,
AND COMPEL THEM TO COME IN, THAT MY HOUSE MAY BE FILLED."
~ LUKE 14:23

George Barna, in his excellent book *Futurecast*,[1] estimated that only half of American Christians share the Gospel with even one unsaved person a year. At this rate, Christianity will die out in less than a generation.

I have been all too afraid to share my faith one on one with skeptics of Christianity. I have tended to assume, if they are not in church, they are not interested and my testimony will offend them.

Even if there are serious issues in the home that need to be addressed by the grace of Jesus, most people will not welcome a stranger knocking on their door. They value their privacy and don't like interruptions by either door-to-door salesmen or evangelists.

I have turned to listening prayer to help answer this dilemma, for I believe God will guide me if I ask, and He will unleash my tongue with the words the listener needs to hear.

Fear of looking Foolish

When I ask for more courage to witness to a lost and dying world, I think I hear Jesus say, *"You must invest yourself in others' lives. Truly care for them and pray for them."*

He reminded me of Dessie Blackburn, the Christian saint who often let me stay at her home when I was in junior high so I could participate in after-school activities. "Aunt" Dessie lived in a tar-paper-covered shack, the faded wallpaper of its interior walls decorated with Scripture and pictures of Jesus, and she insisted on saying grace before we ate our simple supper. I disdained her "religion," yet all the while she was gently leading me to Christ.

As a result of her faithfulness, today I am a solid believer who would shout from the rooftops, "Jesus Christ is Lord!"

The Holy Spirit will never lead us into something foolish. He may, however, lead us to something *others* consider foolish. I think of Gladys Alyward, Hudson Taylor, Brother Andrew, Mother Teresa, and many other heroes of the faith who left their homes and fortunes to follow Christ to the utmost regions of the world. How many of their friends and relatives tried to dissuade them? How did they recognize the still, small voice in their hearts that led them on? Where did their amazing courage come from?

Each of these heroes had an intimate relationship with Jesus, and their hearts were completely yielded to Him. They knew His voice, and none other could interfere.

Street evangelism

Several years ago John Elliott of the Foursquare Church of Hitchcock, Texas, persuaded me to help distribute tracts at Galveston's Mardi Gras. I doubt if many people read the little booklets handed them by the lady with a terrified look on her face!

The streets were strewn with these tracts and appeared useless. However, a few people struggling with alcoholism or other addictions picked up a tract before it was trampled underfoot. The words spoke to their hearts of their need for a Savior and led them to the help they needed. Several pews of John's church are filled every week with men and women rescued because of his courageous ministry.

Another effective street ministry, Montrose Street Outreach, is conducted every Wednesday by Martin and Kim Dale, leaders of YWAM Houston, in an open-air parking lot in downtown Houston, reaching folks who might not ever darken the door of a "traditional" church building. Gang bangers, pimps, prostitutes, drag queens, drug hustlers, etc., attend on a regular basis, and are served a hot meal and other necessities as they listen to the Word.

Martin says, "Missions/Evangelism has to begin with the thought of consistency in service." Twelve years ago, when the ministry began, the Dales knew they had to earn trust. Many who attend say they appreciate the team being there every week. God placed them in this place at this time in history, making a difference in many people's lives through the power of the Holy Spirit.

Joshua, man of courage

God instructed Moses to send twelve men to explore the land of Canaan—the Promised Land flowing with milk and honey. Of these, only two came back with a favorable report (Numbers 13:26-33). With God on their side they could conquer the land.

As a result, only these two were allowed to enter the Promised Land, forty years later (Numbers 14:30). In full sight of their destination, the others wandered...and wandered...and wandered, until they died and their children buried them.

How were Joshua and Caleb so filled with courage? They, like the other Israelites, had seen God's hand open the Red Sea and save them from the Egyptians (Exodus 14:21-22). They had seen manna and quail drop like dew from heaven to feed them (Exodus 16). In the midst of the desert, water sprang from a rock to quench their thirst (Exodus 17:1-7). In their first skirmish with enemies, Joshua defeated the mighty Amalekites (Exodus 17:8-16).

Perhaps it was Joshua's time in the Tent of Meeting (Exodus 22:11), when he soaked in the presence of the Lord, that strengthened him into a man of iron-like courage.

When the day finally came to lead the Israelites into the land promised them, God said to Joshua, "Do not let this Book of the Law depart from your mouth; meditate on it day and night, so that you may be careful to do everything written in it. Then you will be prosperous and successful. Have I not commanded you? Be strong and courageous. Do not be terrified, do not be discouraged, for the Lord your God will be with you wherever you go" (Joshua 1:8-9).

Joshua's secret: consistent meditation on God's Word! The book of Joshua is one of amazing victory after victory. In answer to his prayer, God even caused the sun to stand still for a full day (Joshua 10:13-14).

Finally, the fighting was over. "Not one of all the Lord's good promises to the house of Israel failed; every one was fulfilled" (Joshua 21:45).

And we have the beautiful words he spoke as an old man: "As for me and my household, we will serve the Lord" (Joshua 24:15).

The bravest man of all

The bravest man the world has ever seen is Jesus. As God in the flesh (John 1:1), He knew His destiny. He knew that during the Passover Feast in Jerusalem, A.D. 33, He would be arrested, tortured, and crucified.

Isaiah 50:6-7 is a clear prophecy of Jesus's last weeks: "I offered my back to those who beat me, my cheeks to those who pulled out my beard; I did not hide my face from mocking and spitting. Because the Sovereign Lord helps me, I will not be disgraced. Therefore have I set my face like flint, and I know I will not be put to shame."

A few weeks before Passover, He and His disciples rested safely across the Jordan, out of reach of the Sanhedrin. But He set His face like flint and determined to go to Bethany, just outside Jerusalem. His friend Lazarus had died (John 11:14), and He had a mission at the tomb. His disciples tried to talk Him out of going. They knew the danger. Finally, when they saw He was immovable, Thomas said, "Let us also go, that we may die with him."

Jesus set His face like flint, to experience all the evil the world could throw His way:

◇ Hunger
◇ Exhaustion
◇ Poverty
◇ Sorrow
◇ Rejection
◇ Loneliness
◇ Betrayal
◇ Cruelty
◇ Torture
◇ Mockery
◇ Anguish
◇ Death

Within hours of His arrest, knowing all He would face, He and His disciples sang the Hallel, Psalms 113-118, which included the remarkable verse, "This is the day the Lord has made; let us rejoice and be glad in it" (Psalm 118:24, NKJV).

A little later, He told His disciples, "Be of good cheer; I have overcome the world" (John16:33, KJV).

Be of good cheer!

If He had faced all the evil the world could throw at Him and overcome it, what does that mean for us? Can we, by His blood, overcome it as well?

These words were spoken in the context of the Last Supper, the Passover Meal that Jesus shared with His disciples. He took bread and broke it, and probably prayed the words familiar to all Jews, "Blessed art Thou, Jehovah our God, King of the world, who causes to come forth bread from the earth."

According to Luke 22:19, He "gave it to them, saying, 'This is my body given for you; do this in remembrance of me.'"

Saint Paul adds, "For whenever you eat the bread and drink this cup, you proclaim the Lord's death until he comes" (1 Corinthians 11:26).

My church offers grape juice and pieces of cracker, symbolic of a more formal Eucharist. When I drink these little cups and eat the tiny wafers, am I taking into my body the power to overcome evil that Jesus spoke of?

Is His overcoming blood immunizing me, giving me the strength to stand up to every evil thrown against me?

The Acua Project

Missionaries Jim Elliott, Ed McCully, Roger Youderian, Pete Fleming, and Nate Saint determined to reach the Acua/Waodani, a savage South American tribe in the rain forest of Ecuador, believing that missions work was more important than life. This unreached people were described by anthropologists as the most violent people ever studied.

On January 8, 1956, the men's bodies were found by the riverbank where they had landed their small plane. [2]

The five had been dropping gifts from the air for several months to build a friendly relationship with the savage tribe who had been completely isolated from the outside world, who were disposed to kill any stranger on sight, and who were feared by even their head-hunting neighbors. Nate had found their settlement from the air, and the five developed a plan to fly over it every week and drop gifts as a way of making contact. Nate's sister, Rachel, a Bible translator, had a young Waodani girl living with her, who taught them enough of the language to communicate.

On their fourth flight, they began calling out friendly messages by loudspeaker. Soon the Waodani were responding with gifts of their own: a woven headband, carved wooden combs, two live parrots, cooked fish, parcels of peanuts, and a piece of smoked monkey tail. The tribesmen even cleared a space near their village and built platforms to make the exchanges easier.

After three months of air-to-ground contact, the missionaries decided that it was time for the next step. They located a beach that would serve as a landing strip, and prayerfully, with great care, they landed and set up camp. They had decided to carry guns, but only to scare off an attack. Their unanimous decision was to shoot no one, even to save their own lives. Several Waodani visited the camp and seemed friendly, then left. Then, after several uneventful days, all five were speared to death in a surprise attack.

Over 1800 years ago, Tertullian wrote that the blood of martyrs becomes the seed of the Church. Again, that observation proved its truth. More than a thousand college students volunteered for foreign missions in direct response to the story of the five martyrs, and over twenty fliers from the United States volunteered to take Nate's place.

In a decision that would have been unimaginable to most people, the wives and children of the murdered missionaries moved into the Waodani village and helped to care for them, successfully forging a friendship that transformed all of them. Steve, Nate's ten-year-old son, was baptized in the same river where his father had been killed. The men who performed the ceremony were two of the killers-turned-Christians. One of them has become a beloved "grandfather" to Steve's children.

College missionaries

The moral climate of America has become hardened and deaf to Christ's message. Many college students are openly atheistic and mock those who believe. How can anyone reach these calloused hearts?

Don Miller, author of *Blue Like Jazz,* [3] tells how he and a handful of "closet Christians" enrolled at Reed College, one of the most liberal in the nation. When it came time for the college's annual drink n' drug bust, one of the young men suggested they build a "confession booth" and place it in the middle of the event. But instead of encouraging the unbelieving students to confess their own sins, the Christians would confess to them.

The strange new idea was that these Christians would confess that, as followers of Jesus, they had not been very loving. Instead, they had been bitter, and for that they were sorry. They would apologize for neglecting the poor and the lonely. They would ask the students' forgiveness, and would tell them that in their selfishness, they had misrepresented Jesus on the campus. They would tell the people to come into the booth that Jesus loves them. They would apologize to people for getting in the way of Jesus.

Students came up to them to ask what they were building and were told the Christians would be on campus next day to take confessions, to come see them. Some students said it was the boldest thing they had ever seen.

Their first customer finally appeared, wondering if he was supposed to confess all the sinning he'd done at the bash. When he heard Don asking forgiveness for his failure to represent Jesus well, he was shocked, but he listened. And then he said, "I forgive you." And he meant it.

Don talked with him awhile and told him, "If you want to know God, you can. If you ever want to call on Jesus, He will be there."

When this first student shook hands and left, he told his

friends. Lines formed around the booth to confess. Many people wanted to hug when they were done.

How many hearts were touched by these heroic young people who decided to share their faith with humility and love?

As a beautiful footnote, Don writes of a change in his own heart. He went into the project with doubts and came out believing so strongly in Jesus he was ready to die for Him.

Social media

If people no longer welcome traditional visits by church teams, how can they be reached? The explosion of social media has made possible innumerable ways: Facebook, Twitter, Pinterest, and blogs are all supported by Internet browsers. If a person wants to know something about Jesus, he need only type his question into a search engine like Google or Yahoo, and then choose from the selection on his computer screen.

Billy Graham and Bill Bright saw the Internet as the tool of opportunity to reach the Muslim world for Christ, and they set up the Global Media Outreach (GMO) site (www. globalmediaoutreach.com). Hundreds of new believers send their questions to volunteers, who respond by e-mail with Scriptures, prayers, and words of encouragement.

People in crisis

When we're in a crisis, we're much more open to the Gospel. Sickness, death, addiction—all these and more bring home the truth of our own mortality. We can reach people through prison ministries, hospital visitation, recovery/rehabilitation programs, and more. In my community alone, volunteer activities abound:

Linda Kozar, author of *Babes with a Beatitude,* holds a rather large Bible study in her home (www.babeswithabeatitude. blogspot.com). Every few weeks, the women fill zip-lock bags with a pop-top can of soup or ravioli, a napkin, spoon, bottle of water, a granola bar, and an encouraging Scripture. When they see homeless people begging, they hand them a bag with a smile and "God bless you."

Other friends (http://jesuslovesdancers.com/) take the Good News to Houston's strip clubs, modeling studios, and other sexually oriented businesses. They give the dancers bags filled with a small gift, encouraging Scripture, some type of Christian tract/devotional, a card inviting them to church (with map and service times), and chocolate candy. The bouncers, bartenders, and even some of the male patrons respond, asking for prayer. One Muslim club owner gave them money and wanted to support the ministry.

Many sexual trafficking victims are held and abused in brothels and clubs of our own nation, as well as all over the world. Home of Hope (www.homeofhopetexas.com), among others, offers a safe place for adolescent girls who are rescued from this terrible industry.

Back 2 Basics Ministry(www.B2BMinistry.com) brings the love of God to forgotten teenagers that live on the streets, in shelters, foster homes, and mental facilities by providing consistent healthy loving relationships and addressing individual spiritual, emotional, and material needs. The ministry has recently opened a home for girls and their babies and expects to open a boys' home very soon.

Ask, seek, knock

• Lord Jesus, how can I fulfill Your commandment to go into the world and make disciples?

→ *"Beloved, any one of these venues will offer you an opportunity to lead others to Christ. I will lay one or two upon your heart. Ask what you can do to help. Do not be timid or half-hearted. If money is needed, write a check. If time, be prepared to commit to a regular schedule."*

◇◇◇◇◇◇◇◇◇◇◇◇◇◇◇◇◇◇◇◇◇◇◇◇◇◇◇◇◇◇◇◇◇◇◇◇◇◇

- But Lord, how will I have time and money to do this?

→ *"I am Lord over all, and will supply what you need."*

As a result of this prayer, I began the most exciting and fruitful year of my life, ministering to girls at a residential facility for troubled teens, leading a weekly Bible study and sing-along at a local nursing home, and counseling at a pregnancy crisis center.

"Ask and it will be given to you; seek and you will find; knock and the door will be opened to you. For everyone who asks receives; the one who seeks finds; and to the one who knocks, the door will be opened" (Matthew 7:7).

CHAPTER 18

Overcoming Other Strongholds

IF THE SON SETS YOU FREE, YOU WILL BE
FREE INDEED.
~ JOHN 8:36

As your listening prayer experience grows, you will no doubt find, as I did, areas of your life that you deeply desire to change. The harder you try to transform yourself, the worse these bad habits become. The Apostle Paul described our human dilemma perfectly: "Something has gone wrong deep within me and gets the better of me every time.... Is there no one who can do anything for me?" (Romans 7:21-25, MSG).

And then the words that ring through the ages, giving true hope to our hopelessness: "The answer, thank God, is that Jesus Christ can, and does!"

We are enslaved by our sinful habits—a slavery from which Christ came to set us free (Isaiah 61:1). But this freedom comes with a very steep price. God gave His Son, and He asks in return no less than every area of our hearts.

Most of us carry over some defensive attitudes or escape mechanisms from childhood hurts. Someone has said there is no such thing as a "functional" family. Mine was certainly dysfunctional. One of my personal benefits of listening prayer has been to learn to really love and forgive my parents, my brother, and myself.

However, when I am alone for several days or more, hidden feelings emerge that make me want to crawl into the proverbial hole and pull it in after me. The result is an eating binge (chocolate, if I can find it), computer games, and reading suspense fiction. I can and do waste an entire day or more turning off my brain and emotions—hardly the "abundant life" that Jesus promised. To continue in this way would destroy my body, my Christian fellowship, and my productiveness.

Christian psychologists teach that much sin comes from trying to meet a legitimate, God-given need in any way other than by taking it to God so that He can meet it. I decided to ask Him to help me identify the root of my compulsion.

• Lord, I fell yesterday badly and slipped into my old habits. Please show me what needs I am trying to fill the wrong way."

→*"Beloved, what do you see when you think of yourself as a child?"*

A scene from a terrible year when I was six came into my mind—my parents fighting, my mother sick, my father away working and leaving my mother to care for a farm in the dust bowl of southwestern Kansas, and my older brother blamed for not helping enough.

I saw myself as a little girl longing for love and attention from a too-hard working, angry family who had no time for her. Someone has said, "Every child knows whether he is a darling or a nuisance." I had been very welcome as a baby, but when I grew past the "cute" stage, my parents no longer enjoyed me, and everything I did brought a frown to their faces.

• "I needed companionship, structure, and acceptance. Lord Jesus, show me how to fill these needs with You!"

→*"Even now, you want to run away. Do you feel that urge?*

Let Me come into   those memories. What would it have been like to have had Me in your home?"

It was not hard to imagine a different scene, full of peace and joy as our family responded to His beautiful presence.

- "You would have soothed the anger between my parents. You would have healed Mama's body, and she would have had a joyful spirit. You would have provided our needs so Daddy could stay at home taking care of the cows and pigs himself. You would have even kept the dust away. My brother and Daddy would have had a real father-son relationship."

→*"Do you see why it is so important to make Me head of your home?"*

- "Without You, Lord, people live in hell. We lived in hell. When I am alone, those painful feelings come back."

→*"Will you make Me head of your home now? What will that look like?"*

- "To ask Your advice on everything: What food to fix. How to spend my time and money. A chair reserved for You at the table. My do-list submitted to You. Falling asleep at night while You watch over me. Greeting every phone call or visit with anticipation. Taking every problem to You—living, breathing, working, eating, sleeping, writing—all in the light of Your love. Can we start now?"

→*"Go!"*

That was the beginning of a wonderful time of sensing His presence, remembering the words of the "Breastplate" chant that Saint Patrick wrote almost 1600 years ago:

Christ be with me, Christ within me
Christ behind me, Christ before me,
Christ beside me, Christ to win me,
Christ to comfort and restore me,

Christ beneath me, Christ above me,
Christ in quiet, Christ in danger,
Christ in hearts of all that love me,
Christ in mouth of friend and stranger.

If there are recurring sins in your life, no matter the magnitude, I encourage you to ask God this question: "What needs am I trying to fill?" Write down whatever memories come to mind and let Him guide you to His wonderful healing. If this is too painful to do alone, enlist the aid of a Christian counselor to help you through the process.

CHAPTER 19

Recognizing the Counterfeit

THE MAN WHO DOES NOT ENTER THE SHEEP PEN
BY THE GATE, BUT CLIMBS IN BY SOME OTHER WAY,
IS A THIEF AND A ROBBER.
~ JOHN 10:1

The Easter story, with all its power for transformation, seems to make too little difference in the world. If we believe it's true, it should make **all** the difference! People wouldn't be living ordinary lives if we really believed that Jesus rose from the dead.

Reflecting on this as a newly saved teenager, I vowed never to settle for "ordinary, Sunday-go-to-meeting" religion, but to search for the Real Thing. Even though the cares of everyday life too often captured my attention, a part of me never forgot that promise.

Hadacol Christianity

When I was a child, my fondest memories were of my grandmother's annual visits. Mother and I waited with great excitement until the bus rolled in front of the Guymon Hotel and the gray-haired little lady with the wonderful smile made her way down the steps. Then as soon as the driver unloaded her green suitcase, we all climbed in our Model A Ford and headed for a month of pure joy. Grandma had twelve children and countless grandchildren, but when she stayed with us, she treated me as if I were **special.**

I loved to help her unpack her suitcase, and I remember the big brown bottle that lay on top of her carefully folded flowered housedresses. "Hadacol," I read, curious. "What's this, Grandma?"

"It's a tonic," she answered. "It helps my blood pressure and my arthritis. It also helps me sleep."

I didn't think I had any of those complaints, but I wanted to taste it. "Can I, Grandma, can I?"

"All right, dear. But you won't like it."

She was right. It was the worst-tasting stuff I'd ever had in my mouth. From then on, I just watched as she took two big tablespoons of the awful liquid morning and evening, never missing a dose.

Then one morning the newspaper headlines blared, HADACOL PROVEN FRAUD. This miracle-working concoction was nothing more than alcohol and colored water. As a matter of fact, it was being sold in New Orleans bars by the shot glass. A staunch Baptist, Grandma had never let liquor touch her lips. The bottle quietly disappeared.

I often think of the incident in connection with the counterfeit values that pervade our world. The manufacturer's crime was that, in selling elderly people a worthless remedy, he kept them from spending their money on something that would really help. Even if the "remedy" turned out to be harmless, it was still dangerous. Its use would keep people from taking something that would really make a difference in their health.

There's a lot of "Hadacol Christianity" around today—that which is watered down and useless, but which is packaged to appear as the real thing. Those who fall prey to its claims are not only wasting their money and time, but they also fail to find that which is truly effective—the Gospel of Jesus Christ in its entirety.

Inoculation

Inoculation against disease has saved many lives. The tiny bit of vaccine introduced into our bodies sets up an immune response that prevents a full-blown attack of killer diseases. We may develop a small fever after having been vaccinated, but that goes away after a few days. Then, if we are exposed to the illness, we are safe from its devastating effects.

Satan also practices inoculation. He exposes our children to weakened, watered-down Christianity, so they will never experience the "Real Thing." This, I believe, is one of America's greatest dangers.

Satan is the great counterfeiter. He can and does counterfeit everything that is precious in this world—the more valuable, the more counterfeits. But remember, no one ever counterfeited a three-dollar bill. **The counterfeit proves the real thing, for falsehoods cannot exist without the truth they mimic.** We must not make the mistake of missing a real relationship with our Lord in order to avoid being caught up in Satan's fake religion.

Our only protection against his schemes is to stay close to our Shepherd, immersed in His Word, feeding with His flock, and listening for His voice. The search for God's truth will become the consuming passion of our lives, so that we will find ourselves loving Him with all our hearts, all our souls, all our minds, and all our strength (Mark 12:30).

Struggling with doubt

God is big enough to handle our honest doubts, although He chooses not to make the answers easy to find. Jeremiah 29:13 promises, "You will seek me and find me when you seek me with all your heart." Passionately, we search His Word and study the writings of great Christians who have found Him.

But seeking knowledge can be a trap that leads us into

intellectual pride. Sometimes we Christians try to impress others by talking about the book we are reading, the conference we have attended, or the Bible study we are following. One woman told me she felt inadequate because she could never remember a Scripture reference. It's much more important to know the Author than the address!

Following after knowledge for the sake of gathering information will never produce heavenly wisdom—that which is pure, peace-loving, considerate, submissive, full of mercy and good fruit, impartial, and sincere (James 3:17). We will do far better by applying what we already know. If we do this, we won't be tempted to brag about it. "Do not merely listen to the word and so deceive yourselves. Do what it says" (James 1:22). Otherwise, we can get off track very quickly and our ears become deaf to His voice.

The most important part of our search is applying Jesus's teachings to our lives. He said, "If you hold to my teaching, you are really my disciples. Then you will know the truth, and the truth will set you free" (John 8:31-32).

The Greek word for "know" that Jesus used in this passage is not just an academic knowledge. It's knowledge as a result of perception. As we hold on to His teachings and practice them day after day after day, His truth becomes something we experience, perceive, and integrate into ourselves, and we will **know that we know that we know.**

In Lee Strobel's excellent book, *The Case for Faith,* he stresses, "The more you do this [apply His teachings to life], the more you will experientially be woven into a web of faith."[1] We will have "tasted and seen that the Lord is good" (Psalm 34:8).

Truth affects our hearts

As comprehension of His truth sweeps over us and God touches the emotive center of our lives,[2] we may give way to weeping. Our tears are nothing to be avoided, for these are God's way of helping us descend with the mind into the heart and there bow in perpetual adoration and worship. [3] We also see our lives in God's mirror and are compelled to acknowledge not only our sins but also our sinful nature. Then we must trust 1 John 1:9: "If we confess our sins, He is faithful and just and will forgive us our sins and purify us from all unrighteousness."

The entries in our prayer journals may become damp and smeared with our weeping. In this condition, we can clearly hear the still, small voice that never condemns, but like a loving parent, dries our tears and directs us.

When I was six years old, my mother made the most wonderful chocolate cake I had ever tasted. I would have eaten every crumb, but she was careful to place the uneaten half on top of our dish cupboard out of reach of my small, greedy hands.

The next afternoon, however, I came home from school and found myself alone in the house. Mama was working in the garden, Daddy was at work, and my brother had not yet come home. It was just me and that cake, calling my name, and I could not resist. The only way to reach it was to use the shelves of the freestanding cupboard as a ladder. About halfway up to the forbidden treat, the cabinet overturned and crashed to the floor, hurling dishes and cake everywhere.

Screaming hysterically, I ran for the only one who could help—my mother. She rushed to the house to find what terrible thing had happened. With incredible gentleness, she held me in her arms and dried my tears. Then she and I together cleaned up the mess and picked up all the broken pieces.

Over and over, God shows us this same love. When we give in to temptation and make an inevitable mess, there is only One to whom we can go for help. When we run to God and pour out all our shame and regret, like a loving parent, He dries our tears and helps us pick up the broken pieces of our lives.

Recognizing the counterfeit

In order to recognize the false, we must experience the Real. Banks teach their employees to recognize counterfeit bills by handling real money, over and over, until the sensory nerves in their fingers can instantly tell the difference. The more time we spend with Jesus, the quicker we will recognize the philosophies of this world as false, those which have a form of godliness but deny the power of Christ (2 Timothy 3:5).

One church conducted an experiment in which a number of small children were placed in a separate area from their mothers. Neither group could see the other, but they could hear one another. The women were each given the same identical sentence to read, and the children were instructed to identify their mothers by the sound of their voices. "If it's your mom, raise your hand." One by one, the mothers read the few words. Not one of the children made a mistake. In every case, they could identify their mother's voice.

So it is with our Master's voice. Once our spirits have felt that comforting touch day by day and have received the milk of His Word, we need not be afraid that we will follow another.

I recently saw the film, *March of the Penguins*,[3] and watched in open-mouthed amazement as the father penguins endured blizzards and starvation to incubate ugly, misshapen eggs. Caught up in the drama, I cried out, "Let it go! It's not worth it!"

The angels must have felt the same way as they watched my Savior sacrifice Himself for me—"Let her go, Jesus! She's not worth it!"

After four long months when the mother penguins returned to take over the job of child care, there is a wonderful scene where the father penguin sings to his baby so the chick will always recognize his voice. Did God sing to us as He created us in our mothers' wombs? Zephaniah 3:17 speaks of Him quieting us with His love and rejoicing over us with singing. When we hear that unmistakable voice in our spirits, like the little penguin, our hearts will warm with an old, familiar love.

To whom should we pray?

Many people are willing to talk about God, but stutter when

they speak of Jesus. "God" can mean Elohim, the Creator God. "Yahweh" or "Jehovah" refers to the Personal God. "Jesus" is even more personal, for He is our Savior and Friend. He and the Father are one (John 14:9). There is no other name under heaven by which men and women can be saved (Acts 4:12). Listening prayer helps us move into this wonderful relationship so Jesus's name will be as ready on our lips as that of a loving parent or a dear friend.

Jesus taught us to pray to our Heavenly Father. But He also said we must go through Him, for He is the gate (John 10:1, 7). We are not to pray to angels, nor departed loved ones, nor any "spirit guide" or "companion" that we can conjure up. Many people who do not know Jesus as personal Lord are being led astray into counterfeit religions that abound in today's culture.

Real religion leads us to wisdom, which begins with the fear of Almighty God (Proverbs 1:7). These self-made philosophies refuse to acknowledge Him and instead place human experience and feelings in authority. Leanne Payne warns that these "religions" always reconcile good and evil and assign innocence to sin and sinful behavior—calling it good. She emphasizes, "The only defense against this false philosophy is a true and vibrant Christian spirituality." [4]

Jesus promised that His Holy Spirit would lead us into all truth. If we are submitted to His will, we will recognize and be repulsed by Satan's lies. Job, a man who knew God's voice and could not be swayed by his well-meaning friends, said, "Just like my tongue knows the taste of honey, so my mind recognizes truth when I hear it" (Job 12:11, TLB).

Our protection is given in the sixth chapter of Ephesians—the belt of truth, breastplate of righteousness, shoes of the Gospel of peace, shield of faith, helmet of salvation, and the sword of the Spirit or the Word of God. We need every piece of this armor to stand fast against the devil's schemes.

It's also important for us to be involved in a good church that teaches from the Bible and is led by the Holy Spirit. Too many people feel they can stay at home and watch the services on television. But God's plan is for us to be a part of His flock.

Like a sheep that goes off on its own, isolated Christians can be a target for Satan's wolves.

Test the spirits

The Beloved Apostle warns, "Dear friends, do not believe every spirit, but test the spirits to see whether they are from God, because many false prophets have gone out into the world" (1 John 4:1). To avoid deception, apply these tests:

◊ Does this teaching focus on God, or on me? Self-absorption is a satanic lie that leads into all kinds of sin, morbid introspection, and even demonic activity.

◊ Does this honor Jesus Christ as crucified, buried, and risen to be Lord and Savior of mankind?

◊ Is it teaching me to recognize and repent of sin, or to excuse and cover it?

◊ Does this teaching agree with the Gospel of Jesus Christ in its wholeness (not just an isolated verse or two)? Does it line up with the plumb line of God?

◊ Do my most committed, Spirit-filled friends concur that this is of God?

◊ Will this help me be a better servant of my Lord?

Holiness and love

In our churches today there is a tendency to polarize—either emphasizing holiness to the neglect of love, or love to the neglect of holiness. Francis Schaeffer pointed out the need for perfect balance: "Love without holiness is liberalism; holiness without love is legalism." [5] Both distort and render useless the life-transforming truth that Christ came to reveal.

The more prevalent of these distortions is liberalism—trying to embrace every lifestyle. Embracing the sinner is one thing;

embracing the sin another. The lines between good and evil become blurred, evil is renamed, and there is no repentance. The words Alexander Pope wrote in the 18th century are never truer than today:

> "There is a monster of so frightful mien,
>   As to be hated needs but to be seen;
> Yet seen too oft, familiar with her face,
>   We first endure, then pity, then embrace."

Another dangerous counterfeit too common in our churches today is "feel-good" teaching. Many people have never heard a "hell-fire and damnation" sermon. Our concept of God has become so soft that we think, "Surely He would never send people to hell—except perhaps Adolf Hitler and Saddam Hussein." Here again, our protection against such a warped perspective is immersion in the Word of God.

We must seek God for Himself. There are many spiritual "Pharisees" today who don the cloak of Christianity to impress others, yet have no personal relationship with Jesus. Such a person may be morally upright, but have no compassion for others. Pity their families! Self-righteousness is hard to live with.

Sadly, some people attend church to make business contacts. The atheist who mocked me and unsettled my faith attended a large church every week, even singing in its choir. When I asked why, he replied, "It's good for business."

Ravenous wolves also invade our congregations, looking for young girls and boys to seduce. A young man, away from home in basic military training, was told by his drill instructor, "If you want sex, go to church. You'll find plenty of lonely women."

All of this is, of course, rank hypocrisy. But, again, those who water down His message may be the worst of all, for such weakened Christianity may have immunized an entire generation against the Real Thing. I praise God that a great many of today's youth have overcome this "immunization" and are on fire for Christ and are holding His banner high.

CHAPTER 20

Helping Others Listen

EVERYONE WHO ASKS RECEIVES; HE WHO SEEKS FINDS;
AND TO HIM WHO KNOCKS,
THE DOOR WILL BE OPENED.
~ LUKE 11:10

Listening prayer can be taught a number of different ways. In the two-day retreat I attended, Dave Olson used a number of techniques: worship music, dance, art, lectures, small group practice, and personal prayer journaling. Each segment was intended to help participants experience in a new and mighty way their understanding of God's love for them.

At our Christian retreat, because it is difficult for people to carve much time for their busy schedules, we condensed our listening prayer retreats to one day. Using journalizing, art, music, and small-group sharing, these are the questions we tried to cover:

◇   What does God want me to know?

◇   What hinders me from hearing His voice?

◇   How does He want me to worship Him?

◇   What is His personal blessing for my life?

◊   What Scripture promise is for me?

An evening session

One friend developed an even more practical teaching to instruct groups in evening sessions at his church. After explaining the principles of listening prayer, he asks the congregation to do these things:

1. Stand up and close your eyes. Prepare yourself mentally. Imagine yourself in the throne room of God. How do you feel? Are you scared? Go sit on His lap. He is your Father, and He loves you more than you can imagine. Pray like this: "Father, Papa, I'm not afraid of anything You want to say to me. I love You and trust You. I give You—and only You—access to me now. Come speak to me and minister through me now."

2. Relax. Breathe and relax your muscles. Don't get stressed. Too much pressure can make you miss His voice. Remember, His sheep know His voice (John 10:4).

3. Hug the person next to you. Ask God to give you loving, encouraging words for each other. It is not necessary to be a great orator. It is only necessary to love. "If I speak in the tongues of men and of angels, but have not love, I am only a resounding gong or a clanging cymbal" (1 Corinthians 13:1).

4. Now, look around the room and find the person you know the least and pair up, men with men, women with women. One extra is fine, so that you have groups of two or three.

5. Spend five minutes getting to know and love each other.

6. Be still and listen for Jesus's voice for five to ten minutes.

7. Share one of your own needs with each other, taking about two minutes each.

8. Listen again for His voice, about five minutes. Ask the Holy Spirit to come and give you the words your Heavenly Father would have you speak.

9. Now share with one another what you have felt the Lord say. Be bold and unafraid. The Lord's Word never comes back empty (Isaiah 55:11), but will accomplish its intended purpose. Many times we don't know the purpose of a word until we give it. But if it is of God, it will build up His body, bring us into repentance and a closer relationship with God, and build our faith. His words will be smarter than you are and more loving. They may seem to come out of "left field," but will mow down thoughts that had set themselves against Him.

The Holy Spirit will never go against God's written Word. But when He leads, the secrets of hearts may be laid bare. Many times, those who do not know Jesus will be led to fall down and worship God, exclaiming, "God is really among you!" (1 Corinthians 14:25).

10. Now spend several minutes telling each other what their words have meant to you.

Remember: Don't be frustrated or discouraged. For some, it may take a hundred tries, but this personal communication with Christ is the pearl of greatest price. Listening even to one another is difficult. How often do we continue to talk to people and realize they aren't listening? How many of us can remember the last few words spoken to us from the pulpit? Open our ears, Lord, and teach us to listen!

Results

At Hidden Manna, we encouraged those who came for personal retreats to join us in our morning devotions. While none of us were certified as counselors, we could pray with them and teach them to listen for God's comfort and guidance.

A Bible, an inexpensive notebook, and a pen were all the

tools they needed. All of us read the same Scripture silently and then wrote down what we felt God telling us. Then we read what He had given us and invited them to do the same. While their initial attempts were usually timid, they went back to their rooms with new hope and insight. Often this was the beginning of great healing in their lives.

One woman could not stop weeping on arrival. Three days later, she left with a new outlook on life and renewed hope. This is her report:

"I came here fearful, angry, depressed, and in much physical pain. I walked out courageous, hopeful, joyful, and in very little pain. God ministered to me in a real and personal way. It's been years since I really heard His voice, and it was so awesome. I was ministered to spiritually, physically, emotionally, and in every way made whole again. I feel like a complete person again, and I haven't felt like this in over twenty years. My smile doesn't feel like a mask anymore."

A young man was struggling with memories of many past injustices, and his written words were filled with bitterness. But as he returned to his room, a gust of wind sent dead leaves spiraling down in front of him, and he realized God was telling him to let Him blow away the past. The man's eyes and heart opened, he began to use listening prayer in a mighty way. As he left, he told us he'd been able to let go of the past and was ready to deal with the problems of today.

An older woman seemed so hopelessly depressed that we were afraid a retreat would be of little benefit. However, she began to practice listening prayer, and the difference in her outlook was soon amazing. She called me the evening after she returned home and sounded like a new woman. Her voice was so strong and full of hope and vitality, I had to ask myself, "Is this the same person?" She is now reaching out and teaching others. With her permission, I am sharing the words she recently heard God speak to her heart:

"My Gloria, I am proud of you and your renewed effort to spend more time with Me. As you can tell, it is paying off, and,

as you continue in this way, you are going to see more and more prayers answered. I appreciate your faithfulness, and there will be rewards. You will no longer have to take time out for a depression, losing hard-fought battles for which you have prayed, and losing momentum in the growth of your faith. As you continue to abide in faithfulness to Me, I will provide everything you need for strength, a healthy mind and body, and the ministry for which you have yearned. I love you, My daughter, and indeed, you are a sweet savor to My nostrils."

CHAPTER 21

Encouragement

This has been just a primer on listening prayer. Many others, much more spiritual than I, have written on hearing God's voice and on the benefits of journaling prayers. I have shared my own experiences in my walk thus far, aware that these are but a few baby steps. God's presence is much more real to me now than when I began, and this is the Pearl of Greatest Price I want to share with you.

I pray that you will have found hope and encouragement in these pages, and that God's voice will become as precious to you as it has to me.

May He go with you and surround you with His great love.

Prayer of Commitment

"Jesus, I want to know You personally. Thank You that You sacrificed Your life for me so that I could be right before God. I want You to come into my life. I accept the fact that You are the only one who can give me the power to change and save me from an eternity apart from God. Thank You for the forgiveness that comes through Jesus and for giving me eternal life with God. Take control of my life. Make me the person You created me to be."

Signed_____

Date_____

If you have prayed this prayer with a sincere heart today, I encourage you to sign and date this sheet. Then tell others of your commitment. "If you confess with your mouth, 'Jesus is Lord,' and believe in your heart that God raised him from the dead, you will be saved" (Romans 10:9-10). You are a new creature in Christ, and your name is written in the Lamb's Book of Life.

Find a good church that does not water down the Gospel and where you can feel the love of Jesus radiating throughout

the congregation.

Begin a time of devotions, when God will open His Word to your heart in a way that you can apply it to your life this very day. Use a prayer journal to record your prayers and His direction. Seek a strong Christian friend with whom you can share the insights He gives you.

When your life changes—and it will—I would love to hear from you. You may write me at this address: 15 Still Glen Court, The Woodlands, TX 77381.

May God bless you richly and reveal Himself to you as you seek His voice.

ACKNOWLEDGMENTS

I must thank so many people who stood beside me and helped make this book a reality. In particular, I'd like to recognize Dina Sleiman of WhiteFire Publishing, who saw something of value in the manuscript; my critique partners Linda Kozar and Louise Looney; and my wonderful family. Most of all, I thank my Lord and Savior, Jesus Christ, who reached down and made something worthwhile of my life.

CHAPTER NOTES

[1] Nicky Gumbel. *Questions of Life: A Practical Introduction to the Christian Faith*. Elgin: David C. Cook Publishing, 2002.

[2] David Olson, Listening Prayer Ministries.

[3] *NIV Christian Growth Study Bible*. Grand Rapids: Zondervan, 1997.

[4] Spiros Zodhiates, Th.D., ed. *The Complete Word Study Dictionary, New Testament*. Chattanooga, TN, AMG Publishers, 1992.

[1] Ralph W. Neighbour, Jr. and Jim Egli. *New Believer's Station*. Houston, TX, TOUCH Outreach Ministries, 1995.

[1] Robert Cull. "Open Our Eyes, Lord." Marantha Music, 1976.

[2] David Olson. *Listening Prayer: My Sheep Hear My Voice*. Listening Prayer Ministries, 2000.

[3] Ibid.

[4] Peter Lord. *Hearing God*. Grand Rapids: Baker Books, 2011.

[5] Annie Johnson Flint and Hubert Mitchell. "He Giveth More Grace." Lillenas Publishing Co., 1941.

Chapter 4

[1] Leanne Payne. *The Broken Image: Restoring Personal Wholeness through Healing Prayer*. Grand Rapids: Baker Books, 1995.

[2] Jesse Lyman Hurlbut. *Hurlbut's Story of the Bible*. Philadelphia: John C. Winston Co., 1904.

[3] SBC Bible Pathway Devotional and Bible Reading Program, a method of reading the Bible cover to cover in one year's time.

[4] Ralph W. Neighbour, Jr. *Cover the Bible*. Houston: TOUCH Publications, 1999.

[5] Josh McDowell. *Evidence that Demands a Verdict*. San Bernardino: Here's Life Publications (Campus Crusade for Christ), 1972.

[6] *The Case for Christ, The Case for the Resurrection, The Case for Creation, The Case for Faith*, etc. Zondervan Publishing Co.

Chapter 5

[1] *Christian Growth Study Bible*, study notes by Youth with a Mission. Grand Rapids: Zondervan, 1997.

[2] David Olson. *Listening Prayer: My Sheep Hear My Voice*. Listening Prayer Ministries, 2000; p. 74-75.

Chapter 7

[1] Loren Cunningham and Janice Rogers, Youth with a Mission. *Is That Really You, God?*

Chapter 8

[1] Richard J. Foster. *Celebration of Discipline: The Path to Spiritual Growth.* San Francisco: HarperCollins, 1989.

[2] Ibid.

[3] Peter Lord. *Hearing God.* Grand Rapids: Baker Books, 2011; p 123.

[4] Kathy Ide. "Time to Pray." *Chicken Soup for the Soul of America: Stories to Heal the Heart of Our Nation.* Ed. Jack Canfield, Matthew Adams, and Mark Hansen. Kansas City: HCI Publishing, 2002.

Chapter 9

[1] Website. www.wsws.org/articles/w004/jan2004/debt-j15.shtml.

Chapter 10

[1] *Time.* June 6, 1983: Vol. 121, No. 23.

[2] Mrs. Frank Mayfield. "Fear Not." *The Road of Life.* Canyon: Staked Plains Press, 1984.

[3] Peter Marshall. *Mr. Jones, Meet the Master: Sermons and Prayers of Peter Marshal.* Ed. Catherine Marshall. Revell, 1949.

Chapter 11

[1] Neil T. Anderson et al. *Breaking the Bondage of Legalism.* Eugene: Harvest House, 2003.

[2] Dottie Rambo. "He Looked Beyond My Fault." Heart Warming Music Co. International, 1967.

Chapter 12

[1] Website. http://www.torah.org/features/spirfocus/guilt.html, 11/12/05.

[2] Tony Castle. *The New Book of Christian Quotations.* Crossroads Publishing Company, 1982.

[3] Bill Gothard. "Basic Youth Conflicts." Conference material.

[4] Augustus Toplady. "Rock of Ages." 1776.

Chapter 13

[1] Dorothy Clarke Wilson. *Ten Fingers for God.* New York: McGraw-Hill, 1965.

Chapter 14

[1] Website. http://en.wikipedia.org/wiki/Clinical_depression, 11/05/2005.

[2] Philip Yancey and Dr. Paul Brand. *In His Image.* Grand Rapids: Zondervan, 1984.

[3] Ibid.

[4] Wikipedia. "Clinical Depression."

Chapter 15

[1] Alfred Edersheim. *The Life and Times of Jesus the Messiah.* Grand Rapids: Eerdmans Publishing, 1971.

[2] John Foxe. *Foxe's Christian Martyrs of the World.* Uhrichsville: Barbour Publishing , 1985.

Chapter 17

[1] George Barna. *Futurecast: What Today's Trends Mean for Tomorrow's World.* Carol Stream: Tyndale House, 2011.

[2] Steve Saint. *End of the Spear.* Carol Stream: Tyndale House, 2005.

[3] Donald Miller. *Blue Like Jazz: Nonreligious Thoughts on Christian Spirituality.* Nashville: Thomas Nelson, 2003.

Chapter 19

[1] Lee Strobel. *The Case for Faith: A Journalist Investigates the Toughest Objections to Christianity.* Grand Rapids: Zondervan, 2000.

[2] Richard J. Foster. *Prayer: Finding the Heart's True Home.* San Francisco: Harper, 1992.

[3] Ibid.

[4] *March of the Penguins.* Warner Independent Pictures and National Geographic, 2005.

[5] Leanne Payne. *Listening Prayer.* Grand Rapids: Baker Books, 1999.

[6] Francis Schaeffer. *The Great Evangelical Disaster.* Wheaton: Good News Publishing, 1984.

CPSIA information can be obtained
at www.ICGtesting.com
Printed in the USA
FSOW01n0530151015
12113FS

9 781939 023148